Developing self-conf
in young writers

by Steve Bowkett

B L O O M S B U R Y
LONDON · OXFORD · NEW YORK · NEW DELHI · SYDNEY

Bloomsbury Education
An imprint of Bloomsbury Publishing Plc

50 Bedford Square
London
WC1B 3DP
UK

www.bloomsbury.com

First published in Great Britain 2017

Copyright © Steve Bowkett, 2017
Illustrations in Figures 3.5 and 3.6 copyright © Tony Hitchman, 2017
Thinking Child extracts, p.42 © Sue Dixon
Cover illustrations © Shutterstock, 2017

A catalogue record for this book is available from the British Library.

ISBN
PB: 9781472943651
ePub: 9781472943675
ePDF: 9781472943668

2 4 6 8 10 9 7 5 3 1

Typeset by Newgen Knowledge Works (P) Ltd., Chennai, India
Printed and bound by CPI Group (UK) Ltd, Croydon, CR0 4YY

This book is produced using paper that is made from wood grown in managed, sustainable forests.
It is natural, renewable and recyclable. The logging and manufacturing processes conform
to the environmental regulations of the country of origin.

To find out more about our authors and books visit www.bloomsbury.com. Here you will find extracts, author
interviews, details of forthcoming events and the option to sign up for our newsletters.

Acknowledgements and Dedication

I wish to offer thanks to my long-time friend, artist Tony Hitchman, who has again given generously of his time and skill in creating several of the illustrations in this book.

Thanks also to Katherine and Claire at the Ellis Guilford School & Sports College for involving me in their brilliant 'Write Here, Write Now' project over several years. If every school had the wherewithal to model this great initiative, thousands of students would become more confident writers, with all the attendant benefits that brings in boosting results.

Finally, I dedicate this book to the late Jonny Zucker, an author whose enthusiasm and energy in helping children to become better writers was boundless.

Contents

Introduction

'Anyone who has never made a mistake has never tried anything new.' Albert Einstein

The writer P.G. Wodehouse was once asked if he ever read the reviews of his work. He said, 'No, but I do weigh them.' He recognised that to feel uplifted by positive comments put him as much under the influence of the reviewer as to feel deflated by negative opinions.

This is not a trivial point. Of course we all like to receive some praise, though a single negative comment can undo the good work of many positive ones. A few years ago I was asked to be on the judging panel for a children's writing competition. One of the winners was 16-year-old Ellie who was absolutely delighted with her achievement and told me that her ambition was to be a published author. The following year I met Ellie again. She had not entered the competition this time but volunteered to be one of the helpers at the event. When I asked her how her writing was coming on her face fell and she confessed that she hadn't written anything for months. When I asked why, she told me that shortly after her competition success she handed in a short story to her English teacher who had (unprofessionally in my view) told her that it was 'awful'. To compound the damage, Ellie's teacher hadn't justified her opinion at all but simply littered the work with corrections and suggestions for alternative words and phrases (which is no justification at all).

I wonder if you find this at all controversial? You might well argue that a teacher's job is precisely to improve the standard of their pupils' work. I would agree with that of course, but feel strongly that there are more elegant and helpful ways of going about this; ways that nurture and support a child's emerging understanding – in this case of how language works – without knocking back their confidence and demotivating them to continue trying to improve.

The education system is, perhaps necessarily, built on the premises of competition and comparison. Children's efforts are judged against those of their contemporaries within a given school and across schools. Recent press coverage of the performance of British students in PISA tests (Programme for International Student Assessment) highlights the increasing importance in some people's minds of making comparisons on a global scale. Combined with the political wish to attract 'the brightest and the best' so that we can 'drive up standards' to 'run and fight in the global race', plus repeated insistence that the curriculum should be made more 'rigorous', we see the ethos of comparison and competition intensifying, resulting in greater pressure than ever being placed on teachers and pupils alike.

While I have a view on the use of such metaphors within the lexicon of education, as you may have noticed, it's not my intention to debate the issue. Nor do I deny that learning to use language more effectively requires discipline, determination and resilience. In short, becoming a better writer *per se* is hard work. My central contention is that young writers are more likely to make an effort within a nurturing environment that aims to develop their self-confidence as well as their technical skills. Motivation is closely linked with raised self-esteem – bearing in mind that <u>self</u>-esteem is not predicated solely on the opinions of others, but arrived at also through the considered judgements of the individual themselves.

The aims of this book therefore are to give pupils some tips, techniques and strategies for improving the quality of their writing and speaking while also offering advice on dealing with the emotional aspects of developing the craft of 'wordmanship'. The activities are grouped under several broad headings that form a loose sequence of study should you decide to work through them in order. On the other hand, you might choose to cherry pick certain activities and build them into your own programmes of work. Either way, the intention is that they should complement what you already do to develop your pupils' writing ability in a way that is congruent with the demands of the curriculum, bearing in mind however what Aldous Huxley said that, 'Writers write to influence their readers ... but always, at bottom, to be more themselves'.

Chapter 1
Creating the writing environment

Some years ago, I wrote a few books of short stories about a group of friends who called themselves the Double Darers. They enjoyed daring each other to do things, but whoever made up the dare was then double dared back by the others. Once that happened, everyone in the group had to undertake the dare. If you didn't, you were a yellow-belly chicken, and if you were a yellow-belly chicken three times you had to leave the group, which nobody wanted to do because they all had such fun. Despite their mischief, the Double Darers had a code of honour that was enshrined in two mottoes:

Dare to do it and do your best – with the intention that your best in the future will be better than your best today!

Have fun but hurt no one.

These seem like a good starting point for establishing a learning environment that takes account of various factors which can inhibit children's willingness to write and affect their self confidence.

Factors inhibiting learning and quick solutions

1. **A fear of the blank page**. Feeling anxious that you won't be able to think of anything to write. A lack of strategies for generating, organising and refining ideas.

   Solution: Lots of the techniques in this book will help to overcome the fear of the blank page, but a quick and effective ploy is to ask open questions – Where and when is the action set? What do my characters look like? Why do they do what they do (what is their motivation)? and so on. The same technique works for non-fiction – What points do I want to make and in what order? Where can I check my facts? Who am I writing for (style, age range)? etc.

2. **An over-emphasis on technical accuracy from the outset**.

   Solution: Aiming to be technically accurate is important, but this is a network of skills that grows over time and should not be allowed to inhibit the creative flow when writing or any inhibit child's enjoyment of turning thoughts into words and sentences. Perhaps rather than 'technically accurate', 'technically appropriate' is more important, by which I mean suiting the form and style of the writing to the writer's purposes. If, for example, a child is writing a story where one character is texting another, it would be appropriate to say:

A: 'shaL I cum round tonight?' **B:** 'yS c U bout 6 & we c%d watch a mvie' (though hardly accurate in terms of 'standard' English). A related idea to consider is the degree to which formal knowledge of grammar helps to develop a young writer's skills rather than just existing as a collection of dry facts about language. I've been a published writer for over 30 years and have loved writing for much longer than that, without ever knowing what a fronted adverbial is (or whether it's correct to end a sentence with 'is'). That said, when children are enjoying the act of writing and feel they have something meaningful and interesting to say, they may be more inclined to want to know more about the technical aspects of how language works. The writing itself serves as the context and platform for learning more about grammar and punctuation.

3. **The problem of 'overwhelm'**, where a child is trying to do everything correctly at the same time with the result that the spontaneity of the writing is lost altogether, alongside the very real pleasure of being 'in the zone' when the language flows.

   Solution: One way of solving the problem is to flag up one or two things that you'd like the children to bear in mind as they write, but beyond that, just encourage them to have fun with their writing. So you might ask the class to remember full stops at the end of sentences and to tag each character in a story with a couple of descriptive details e.g. Going back to my Double Darers; Brian was a big, square-looking kid with a big, square head and not much of a neck. He stood like a wall. Kevin had long, sticky-out hair and a wild look in his eye. We used to call him the Mad Professor. If some children forget about capitalising proper nouns (which you reminded them about last week), then this should not become an issue. Whenever did learning look like a curve? This strategy can be used with *selective marking*, where you don't attempt to correct or comment on every error or area for improvement, but only those things that you want the children to remember. This is not laziness; it saves you valuable time and avoids giving back work peppered with corrections, which can be very disheartening. (I well remember my own sense of failure as a child when my exercise book was returned covered in red pen marks. Even worse was when, on the odd occasion, my teacher hadn't even bothered to do that but just put a red line across every page followed by the comment 'Do it again!'. Wouldn't happen nowadays.)

   Another ploy is to remind the class that there are three parts to creating a piece of writing: the thinking time, the writing time and the looking back time. The thinking time is just that, a quiet period when children gain at least a general sense of what they want to say, if not a detailed plan. Having an overview gives them a helpful sense of direction and dampens the tendency that some of them have when writing to grab at the first thought that comes to mind. In my experience boys, more than girls, suffer from 'Snatched Thought Syndrome', which all too often gives rise to writing full of clichés and derivative ideas, obvious rather than fresh vocabulary, and wild and wacky ideas unsupported by any rationale for their use. Asking children to plan the direction of their writing also gets them out of the habit of trying to compose the general structure of the work at this stage. Some children will attempt to write the story or essay when all you want is for them to gather ideas and give them some degree of order. Writing 'from cold' leads many children to make it up as they go along and means that redrafting becomes more of a chore whereas forming a plan, with the writing following on some time later, allows children to assimilate their thoughts. This occurs largely at a subconscious level and gives rise to that lovely feeling of good ideas 'coming out of the blue' and fitting together when the writing itself is happening.

4. **Over formulaic instructions**. While planning is important, writing in accordance with too many instructions can inhibit the creative flow and stifle the freshness of the work.

    Solution: General guidance such as using the well-known 'story hill' or advising children to use shorter sentences to increase the pace of a story is useful, but insisting that, for example, the first sentence must be five words long and that children must use a variety of verbs instead of 'said' tips the balance too far. In the same way that selective marking focuses on one or two aspects of the work, you might ask children to bear one guideline in mind as they write, making sure that it's a support and not a straightjacket.

5. **Fear of failure**. This is the central issue around which the others orbit; the anxiety created by thinking that you're not good enough, coupled with being unfavourably compared with your contemporaries and/or against some externally imposed set of criteria.

    Solution: There isn't a quick solution but the ideas in this book aim to help. Bear in mind the advice that every word you write is another step towards becoming a better writer. Even very successful writers are still learning and, sometimes, writing simply doesn't turn out as you want it to. It all counts as making progress.

How can we help our students?

We would all like to see literacy levels rise, for students to leave formal education being able to communicate confidently and effectively; to be creative, independent thinkers who can express themselves clearly and who are less likely to be influenced unwittingly by the bias and rhetoric of others. If some of those students leave school with a love of writing (and reading) for its own sake, then that is a bonus of which we can all be justly pleased.

So how might we accomplish this?

Attainment and achievement

A few years ago, I met 11-year-old Billy at summer school. He was one of a number of children coming up from primary school into Year 7 and had been invited to a week of enrichment activities to help boost his literacy. He had been struggling with his writing for years. At first Billy was cocky and disruptive, wanting to be the centre of attention and often interrupting the storytelling session I ran as a precursor to the writing workshop proper. (I'm sure you'll realise as I did that this was all 'front'; that Billy's attitude was a defence mechanism because he felt vulnerable, even threatened, in thinking he would be asked to do something at which he would fail. He settled as time went on however, and gradually came to feel more comfortable, in part due to some of the techniques mentioned here.)

By mid-morning we were ready for our first task, writing a simple description of a picture. Billy took himself off and spent half an hour hunched over his notebook, his left arm curled protectively around it so that nobody could see what he was doing. His teacher mentioned how pleased she was that he was willing and able to concentrate for so long. When he showed her his finished piece, she gasped. I could see that Billy's work was barely legible, incoherent in places, randomly punctuated and badly spelt. Also, he had not written much of a description but rather a story featuring the person in the stimulus picture.

'That,' she told him, 'is amazing. I've never seen you sit down and concentrate for so long Billy. And look, you've written over three pages and produced a finished story. Well done.'

Shortly afterwards, we persuaded Billy to read his story to the group. He did so haltingly and he often needed help from his teacher. But when he finished, the other children burst into a spontaneous round of applause and Billy glowed with pleasure and pride.

The point is, though Billy's work would earn a low attainment score, his achievement in creating it was huge. Here was a child who, more often than not, would fly into a temper when asked to do some written work in the classroom – either that or stubbornly and sullenly refuse to pick up his pen. Yet here he had given up a day of his summer break, knowing that he was going to be asked to write and be judged by his classmates, and he had tried. He had dared to do it and had done his best. While the technical quality of Billy's work may not have improved greatly by the end of the day, there was no doubt that his attitude towards writing had changed significantly and for the better. As the author Ian Fleming said, effort is desirable for its own sake; everyone must try. He regarded those who succeeded by their own endeavours as heroes (displaying noble qualities like patience, determination and resilience) – though we must qualify success in terms of achievement as well as of attainment.

The continuum of attainment

Do you, as I do, sometimes see criticism of the so-called 'everyone is a winner' attitude to children's learning where people are reluctant to tell any child that they have failed? On the other hand, when I was at school, all pupils in any class were put in strict rank order for various subjects based exclusively on test scores; so my report might read 6/30 English, 18/30 PE, 26/30 Maths (invariably followed by my teacher's comment 'Could do better!').

Two important ideas for gaining a perspective on this issue are multiple intelligences and the plasticity of intelligence.

Multiple intelligences

The notion that people are intelligent in different ways is now commonplace. The concept of multiple intelligences was developed by Professor Howard Gardner of Harvard University in the early 1980s. Children who have the evolving ability to manipulate language are 'linguistically intelligent', while those who have an aptitude for maths are 'numerically intelligent' and so on. This concept suggests that the traditional view of intelligence, based usually on I.Q., is limited. Children's intelligences will develop at different rates based on many factors, not least the degree of motivation in a child to learn in any given area. The importance of cultivating motivation (i.e. increasing children's 'emotional intelligence') is highlighted by Professor Carol Dweck of Stanford University in a number of books such as *Self Theories* and *Mindset*, in which she offers strategies for empowering people to succeed.

Plasticity of intelligence

Professor Gardner's model also highlights the 'plasticity' of intelligence – the fact that intelligence is both multi-faceted and a process, not a fixed state but instead an evolving set of capabilities. We all know children who have struggled with their learning only to flourish upon reaching a certain age, the mental equivalent of a growth spurt.

Taking a realistic view of what a child can do, coupled with cultivating a desire to improve, supports an attitude of self-confidence, dampening the tendency to think 'I'm no good at this' and, equally, discouraging the establishment of self-inflated arrogance masking a deeper fear of failure. In terms of writing, all authors stand on what might be called the 'continuum of attainment'. I accept that there are authors who write more powerfully or profoundly than I do and those who are more commercially successful. Equally, I can acknowledge that I am a more successful author than others, including those whose work I've read and those who have never had any material published. Again, this is to do with attainment. Realistically, in terms of my writing, I am not at the top of the class but neither am I at the bottom.

A linked insight is that we can be better at some types of writing than others. While I might hope to write a reasonable fantasy story, I wouldn't (at the moment) make a very good job of a Western. Similarly, I have been pleased with some of the science fiction I have written but feel I couldn't attempt a creditable piece of historical fiction. The same is equally true of non-fiction. Thus I can enjoy staying in the comfort zone of doing what I think I can do well, while relishing the challenge of trying new things just to see what's possible – moving into the so-called 'stretch zone'.

So in establishing a supportive writing environment for children, as much as possible we can create opportunities for them to write what they enjoy and are already good at while encouraging them to explore and experiment with new forms so that they can incorporate new information or a more difficult skill. This attitude of being willing to try (and try new things) while adopting a realistic view is powerful. Children can be credited for taking note of their strengths as much as where they think they can improve; accepting that there will always be 'better' writers while recognising that this does not diminish any child's achievement when they dare to do it and do their best.

Two powerful motivators

Two powerful motivators are quick feedback and sincere praise. When we ask children to undertake a thinking/writing task it's important that through our spoken and written comments we keep them informed; letting them know they're doing fine when that's the case and prompting them to think further when things are not going so well or they appear to be struggling.

Sincere praise has to be just that and not false flattery: children will spot this at once. It's also wise to apply the 3PPI formula, which is, as far as possible, to find three points of (sincere) praise for each area we spot that needs improvement. The reason for this is that there is great psychological power in mentioning something three times. The first point of praise might be a fluke, the second could be coincidence, but when a child hears that third positive comment, he's convinced that he's doing something right.

These two simple techniques usually 'encourage' children to have a go and stick at it. And I think it's useful to read that word as 'en-courage', to give courage to someone where it may not have existed before.

Value the thinking

Many schools now pride themselves on being 'thinking schools', where thinking skills are taught explicitly and consistently by all staff through all years and across all subject areas. An extension of thinking skills' programmes in such schools is the development of philosophy for children where the establishment of communities of enquiry serves to consolidate a network of skills that can then be applied in all other areas of the children's learning. These skills include:

- listening
- sharing thoughts with others
- creating ideas of your own
- explaining ideas in greater depth
- responding to other people's ideas
- developing other people's ideas
- observing
- defining
- asking questions
- clarifying
- making distinctions
- giving examples and counter examples
- spotting patterns
- creating overviews
- making generalisations.

There are many more, but even this small selection highlights the fact that as children learn how to use these skills flexibly and in combination, their learning generally, and their mastery of language, can only improve.

Top tip
For more information on thinking schools, go to www.thinkingschool.co.uk. For more information on thinking skills and their use in philosophy for children, type 'assessment of philosophical skills by Clare Douglas' into your search engine.

As well as 'thinking' having great value in education, in order to develop children's self-confidence as writers we also need to value their thinking. This applies even to a first snatched thought (see Snatched Thought Syndrome, page 4) or an idea that as adults we realise is derivative and unoriginal. The ethos of the classroom needs to reflect the worth we place on children's ideas. As we establish this ethos children will increasingly be prepared to offer their thoughts and are less likely to be discouraged when we ask them to think further or come up with alternative ideas.

Comment on the writing not the writer

Children must come to understand that your comments and attainment scores refer to the writing itself and not to them as people; in other words that they should not take things personally. This is sometimes a hard lesson for young writers to learn. Even experienced adult writers can feel crushed and 'rejected' when a publisher declines a cherished piece of their work. In this context it has been said that a book is the writer's heart in someone else's hands, though publishers will see it as a product that hopefully will generate some profit.

It's natural that some children feel frustrated if they think their work is not very good, and equally will be disappointed when you point out what needs correcting and highlight areas that need to be improved. Such emotions, however, can be seen as indicators of a child's desire to do well – see the section Dealing with feelings (page 19).

Try the 'graphic equaliser' activity

Here you encourage children to take a more detached view of their performance across different areas of writing, assessing themselves honestly for things they know they can do well and for areas that need improvement. Give each child a template to fill in, suggesting a different colour or style of shading for each column.

Spelling	Punctuation	Plotting	Characters	Dialogue	Pace and Tension

FIG 1.1   The graphic equaliser

Note that the graphic equaliser can be used with broad subjective comments such as, 'I'm not very good/pretty good/very good at this' etc. or with reference to more specific and measurable parameters relating to curriculum levels.

Diamond ranking

Another way of helping children to assess their own performance is to introduce the idea of diamond ranking. Give out scraps of paper to each child, ask them to jot down different aspects of their writing on the scraps and then to position them in order of how well they think they can do those things. Two or more scraps can be placed on a level with each other if a child thinks he performs equally well in those areas.

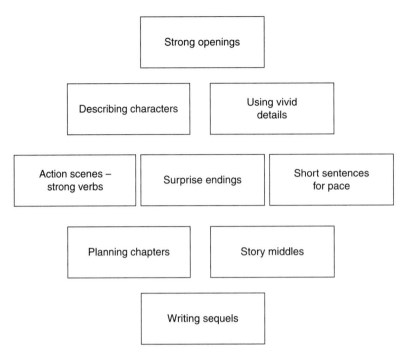

FIG 1.2   Diamond ranking

The rankings do not have to be as regular and formal (i.e. strictly diamond shaped) as in the figure above; less symmetrical positioning will allow for more flexible and subtle assessments. The technique can also be used for non-fictional forms of writing.

Graphic equaliser templates can be filed: when the activity is run again weeks or months later, children will be able to judge their progress. Diamond rankings can be photographed for the same purpose of comparison.

Sharing advice

As part of the establishment of a supportive writing environment, ask children to write down tips for good practice based on what they can already do well. These might be concerned with the technical aspects of the language or good working habits and a positive attitude towards writing. Post them up on a 'good writing' display board. Similarly, let the children know it's OK for them to ask advice from their classmates when there are aspects of their writing they want to improve. Extend this strategy by looking at short stories/extracts from longer works by published authors to see 'how the experts do it'.

Most children who enjoy reading will have favourite books or authors. Run discussion sessions where children can explain why they like a particular story or series so much. Encourage participants to back up their opinions as far as they can. Introduce a more analytical approach as necessary. A child might say he liked the way an author described a character because he could see that person clearly in his mind. You might then add to that point by mentioning vivid adjectives, strong metaphors, the use of dialogue to give the character depth, and so on.

Annotated stories

Develop children's willingness and ability to assess stories and other forms of writing by giving them templates where they can note their impressions of their own and others' work. Many traditional tales are in the public domain; the text can be freely downloaded and pasted into the template. And if you don't think this is sacrilegious, remove sample pages from a book, paste them on to a large sheet of paper so that children have room to note their observations and questions. Handwritten pages of the children's own work can be used in the same way, though if they are working on computers, the process becomes much easier. For more stories and worksheets, see **Bloomsbury Online Resource 1A**.

First impressions:		Questions and other notes:
Elegant Dracula with red silk-linked cape. Slicked back black hair.	The skeleton tripped over Dracula's polished shoe and went sprawling on to the grass. With a shriek of delight the vampire swirled up his cloak, turned and ran away through the trees.	Are there other people nearby? I imagine a park. Characters are going to a party.
Wet grass, glinting. There's a street lamp not far away.	"Hey come back! – Diana yelled after him. "We've got a bone to pick with you!"	Quite a friendly feel to things. Dracula was just up to mischief.
Oak trees, leaves falling. Lots of leaves on the ground.	Eleanor Trent burst into giggles but the skeleton – actually Tommy Hyatt who lived on Acker Street – groaned and winced and held his aching back as he scrambled stiffly to his feet.	Tone is comedy, light hearted fun.
Diana – red hair, strong face.		What costumes are Diana and Eleanor wearing?
	"I suppose," he said, "you think that's funny?"	
Eleanor – younger looking, thinner, blonde hair with red and purple streaks for Halloween.	Eleanor tried to force herself to stop, but the giggles came bubbling up like soda and she had to put a hand over her mouth to hide her mirth. Diana just grinned, and it was such an open friendly grin that Tommy could do nothing but shrug and instantly forgive her.	Friendly feel.
Tommy – a couple of years younger (about 12), short with straight dark hair, skeleton body costume.		What sound does the wind make in the trees?
Windy. Moonlight. Rushing clouds.	"OK, so it was kind of funny..." He dragged off his skull mask. Eleanor thought that his flushed face and tousled hair looked really cute.	What is the smell of the wet leaves and grass?
	"Thank you kind ladies for helping a poor old bag-o-bones on this wild and weird night!"	

FIG 1.3 Annotated stories

These various strategies presuppose that you allow 'looking back time' as part of the writing process. The two core questions children can ask when reviewing their work are:

- What do I need to change to make this the best I can do today?
- What have I learned by writing this that will help me to improve as a writer?

Asking these questions may be a precursor to redrafting or an aspect of a child's self-assessment after they have finished the project and regard the writing as 'polished'. Even when a writer feels they have completed a piece, reviewing it later usually throws up a few things that they would now wish to change. To paraphrase Leonardo da Vinci, 'A story is never truly finished, only ever abandoned.'

Once again, looking at work months later will give children a perspective on how far they have improved in the meantime. The more changes they would make to a past piece of writing, the more they realise how much more experienced they are now.

The diamond of success

Years ago, I came across an idea called 'the triangle of failure'. Imagine a triangle with 'ability' written above the peak and 'imagination' and 'nerve' placed at the other two points. Sometimes what inhibits the development of a child's ability, or what is perceived as a failure of ability, is actually a failure of imagination and/or nerve.

A failure of imagination might simply be that a child has never envisaged success, perhaps through limiting self-beliefs. Or it may be that they do not yet have the strategies available to make the most of their imagination. A failure of nerve is a state of 'I dare not try this', for the various reasons we've already touched on – a fear of being unfavourably compared with classmates, getting a low mark etc.

If issues can be addressed at these deeper levels of imagination and nerve (which is what this book is about), then the triangle is transformed into one of success: the child and others realise they had the ability after all and/or that their potential is increasingly on the way to being fulfilled.

A powerful way of ensuring this is to add the component of 'will', thus turning the triangle into a diamond. In this case, will means creating a sure sense of direction and destination, driven by clearly imagined intentions and sustained self-determination. The vision comes first: this is where I am now and this is where I intend to be. The destination might be to finish a particular project or the more general desire to improve as a writer (though it's important to be clear about what 'being a better writer' looks and feels like). Applying strategies for empowering the imagination and strengthening the nerve – i.e. cultivating robust self-confidence and a degree of heightened self-esteem – generates a sense of meaningful progress.

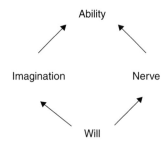

FIG 1.4   Diamond of success

Effort, resilience and determination must follow, though these are supported by the other points of the diamond, which leads to the successful completion of tasks on the journey to fulfilling one's potential.

Emergent understanding

This might be an obvious idea to some but will result in a change of perception for others; the realisation that children are *learning* to be writers and that what we perceive as errors are often indications of a growing understanding. If a child writes *seperate* instead of *separate*, we could say that he had spelt the word wrongly, or we might acknowledge that he got it seven out of eight correct. He is on the way to getting it right. Similarly, when we read 'Tony put the book back in its' right place on the shelf', we could say that *its'* is wrong and that it should be *its*, but we can also appreciate the fact that the child has grasped the idea of possession linked to apostrophes.

Recognising emergent understanding should not prevent us from correcting errors, though it might make us as educators and the children as learners more tolerant of them.

The learning value of mistakes

The notion of emergent understanding is one example of the learning value of mistakes, in this case that the errors also reveal that a child is on the way to greater understanding and accuracy.

When I ask children to write, I tell them not to scribble over any errors or alterations they make, but rather just to put a line through them so that we can see their 'workings out'. I combine this with emphasising that it's fine to change your mind; that to have our best ideas, we need to have many ideas; and that a change of mind also indicates reflectiveness and the ability to make a judgement and reach a decision. It's also true that, as the old saying has it, 'Good decisions come from experience and experience comes from bad decisions' (attributed to Mark Twain).

Mistakes can also flag up bad learning habits and/or inefficient working methods. The absence of full stops at the end of sentences in a child's work might point to a current lack of understanding of that punctuation mark or hurried reviewing of the work during looking back time. It might also indicate an inability to concentrate during writing or suggest simple laziness. Whatever the reason, the willingness to acknowledge mistakes and learn from them is in itself a positive quality.

Fixing problems

The author Douglas Hill, who was a close friend of mine, recognised that even experienced authors don't always – or even often – produce a finished product after a first or second draft (or even more). Sometimes a short story or novel seems to appear as though by itself: the writer is 'in the zone' and the language flows. This is a very satisfying and uplifting experience. Even so, upon rereading, it's clear that the work will need to be 'tweaked' and 'polished' before it is (as da Vinci said) 'abandoned' and the author moves on to the next project. What seemed a well-crafted sentence at the time of writing might look clumsy or overwritten the next day (or whenever the author comes back to the piece after letting it 'cool off'). It's also possible that an idea pops to mind for a much better way of framing a thought – a completely different sentence that might do the work of several previously written. Insights about improving the piece come along at a deeper structural level too rather than just at a paragraph, sentence or word level. Sometimes a writer will realise that entire scenes or chapters need to be rewritten, or that the whole novel or short story is not turning out as it should and needs to be rethought. That an author is prepared to think again and undertake a rewrite is a marker of their professionalism and flags up the fact that, as writers, we never stop learning – thus putting the lie to the old saying that 'practice makes perfect', though invariably it makes *better*.

Even for young and relatively inexperienced writers, crafting a piece if work can be an emotional labyrinth. As well as the doubts and worries already mentioned there is the sometimes tacit understanding that when children write at school, they are writing primarily for their teachers and against the competitive-comparative ethos that characterises the educational system. All too often, they are also given highly prescriptive writing tasks and limited times to carry them out – I've spoken with many published authors who confess that they would quake at the thought of having to sit a writing exam.

Despite all of this, we serve children best by emphasising the pleasure of writing, rooted in the need we all have to express ourselves clearly and meaningfully. Douglas Hill would always talk about 'fixing problems' when it came to redrafting or polishing a piece of work, and I was always impressed by this. Notice how the idea of fixing problems presupposes that they *can* be fixed, that the work is always salvageable, however dissatisfied or disappointed the writer seems to be with it at the time. Framing the task of rewriting in this way also avoids negative judgements like the piece is 'not good enough', 'useless', 'much worse than my friend's' etc. Encouraging the problem-fixing mentality dampens the tendency towards negative self-talk and injects a sense of purpose into the looking back time that is a vital part of the writing process.

The same optimistic attitude is further supported by the notion of recycling; the understanding that an idea, phrase, sentence, character, event or whatever is ultimately changed or discarded during the writing of one piece of work can often be used in another. No idea is ever really wasted. It is equally true – and a message that needs to be forcefully brought home – that every word a child writes is another step in the direction of becoming a better writer.

So when helping children to look back over their work, you might usefully say to them, 'So can you spot any problems and if so, how can we fix them?'.

Model the behaviour

When I set children a writing task, I sit and write too. Not only that, when as a class we discuss the writing, I mention the difficulties I had; the right word that just wouldn't come to mind, the realisation that I should have written in the first person and not the third, the fact that I introduced a character on page one and then failed to mention him again…

'Modelling the behaviour' amounts to more than just teaching the literacy syllabus or telling the children what a healthy attitude towards writing looks like. At the heart of the 'writing environment' is our willingness as teachers to get involved too; to realise, as the children do, that writing can be a great pleasure but that it's also hard work, a process full of frustrations as well as delights.

A community of writers

The most powerful influences on children's learning are those features of good practice that are embodied in school policy and applied consistently by all staff. Thinking schools, mentioned earlier (page 7), only work because the whole school gets behind the initiative and works together to ensure its success.

The same is true of what we might call 'writing schools', where the requirements of the national curriculum are accepted but where the understanding exists that cultivating a love of writing amounts to more than going through the motions or naming all the parts.

We've spoken of the 'ethos' of a school in the context of writing. The word comes from Greek and means the defining character or spirit of a community or culture. Thus the ethos of a group of people is subtle as well as powerful. Also it is organic in the sense that it is not 'mechanical'; it cannot just be bolted on to what already exists in an institution. It grows and flourishes over time. The organic nature of an ethos also presupposes that everyone contributes usefully to the health and success of the whole, in the same way that every leaf of a tree contributes to the life of the tree.

A writing school is a place where a love of writing is cultivated by all and where everyone contributes towards that goal. It is not a collection of disparate individuals, some of whom are teaching writing and the rest learning about it. Nor is it just about 'raising the bar' to produce a 'literate workforce'. In my mind there is no doubt that people who can express themselves creatively and effectively (whether by writing or through some other means) are often emotionally healthier, more self-determining and more fulfilled than those who have no positive outlet for their thoughts and feelings. Children who learn to write well enjoy many benefits, not just in terms of raised self-confidence and heightened self-esteem but also because their whole outlook is one of curiosity: the ability to ask incisive questions; the will to find out more and reflect upon what they discover; the desire to share ideas and be prepared to modify their own. In short, young writers who enjoy what they do become better learners. Ideally of course, writing becomes a long term passion allowing them to say, as Douglas Hill did when asked if authors make a living, 'Not all authors do, but every one of them that I've met has made a life.'

Publishing projects

The development of technology and the proliferation of self-publishing companies offering print-on-demand facilities make it relatively easy and inexpensive to publish children's work professionally. Various models are possible depending on time and money available and the number of young writers who are involved.

Huxlow Science College and Irthlingborough Junior School in Northamptonshire published a children's novel written by a group of students known as the Ink Links. They worked collaboratively on both text and artwork and the book, *Reflections of Evil*, was produced by AuthorHouse (www.authorhouse.com). The inclusion of an ISBN number (ISBN 978-1-4772-5044-0) – which the publishing company can arrange – means that the title can be sold through retail outlets. The crop of glowing reviews that the story has picked up online will undoubtedly boost the children's confidence even more!

'Write Here, Write Now' was an equally inspired project masterminded by Katherine Davison and Claire Greasby at the Ellis Guilford School & Sports College in Nottingham. All Year 8 students were invited to take part, attending a 'kickstart' session by author Jonny Zucker. The sixty that signed up to the project were split into three groups, each led by a different author; Helen Pielichaty, Emma Pass and myself. Each of us chose a different theme (heroes, science fiction and ghost stories) to develop over the course of four sessions: three in-school workshops and a fact-finding day out. Once the book was printed, students who had contributed were presented with a copy at the launch event to which they, their parents and teachers were invited.

Under the guidance of author Lisa Spencer-Arnell (www.lisaspencerarnell.com), pupils at Lambley Primary School near Nottingham contributed to a project called *Confidence for Kids by Kids* (ISBN

978-1-78003-737-0). The book consists of anecdotes by the children themselves, activities such as wordsearches, letters-to-yourself and a confidence checklist, plus words of advice from, among others, entrepreneur Richard Branson, ex-prime minister David Cameron, TV presenter Sian Williams, and director and actor Emma Clayton. As well as being a practical manual for doing just what the title says, the book represents an ideal way of helping children to boost their self-confidence and raise self-esteem. The book is available as an eBook or paperback via the dedicated website www.confidenceforkidsbykids.com. Profits from sales are being donated to ChildLine.

Patron of Reading

This is a relatively new initiative for forging closer ties between schools and children's authors, who agree to work with the school for a period of approximately three years to raise the profile of reading for pleasure with pupils, parents and staff. Patron of Reading schools agree to invite the author in on a regular basis (at least one visit per year), encourage children to read the author's books and give feedback on them. In return, the chosen author agrees to send a couple of copies of each new published book, contribute to the school newsletter, blog etc., and share ideas regarding reading, books and libraries. Further details of the Patron of Reading collaboration and details of how to join the scheme can be found at www.patronofreading.co.uk.

A writer's pact

Many schools display a list of pupils' rights and responsibilities as part of its ethos of maintaining standards of good conduct. A writer's pact is drawn up along the same lines. In trying to establish a supportive classroom environment where children's thinking and writing can flourish, you have already acknowledged that they have certain rights, which may relate to physical surroundings and will certainly touch upon the way the children behave towards others and others towards them.

By the same token, a writer's pact (from the Latin *pactum* meaning 'something agreed') incorporates the recognition by the children that they carry certain responsibilities for their own learning – and of course we as teachers take our own responsibilities for that very seriously.

As a way of consolidating what has already been said in this book, consider drawing up a writer's pact with your class. What rights do the children feel they can expect from you and from their classmates in their efforts to become better writers? On the other side of that coin, what responsibilities should they honour as a way of earning those rights? If this activity is run across several classes, ideas can be compared and contrasted as a way of creating a writer's pact on which most people can agree.

Here are some ideas. As young writers we have:

- the right to learn to think for ourselves; to listen to advice and decide whether and how it can best help us.

- the right to make mistakes, because we are still learning. But mistakes also help us to learn further if we think about them carefully.

- the right to change our minds. This means that we have thought about our writing and decided on ways of improving it.

- the right to learn in our own way, as far as this doesn't hinder someone else's progress. What works well for one person may not work so well for another.
- the right to be proud of our achievements. When we have tried hard, whatever other people think our efforts can give us pleasure.

As young writers we have:

- the responsibility to try our best and work hard to fulfil our potential.
- the responsibility to respect other writers, helping them where we can and not doing anything to slow their learning down.
- the responsibility to earn the respect of others.
- the responsibility to listen to others who have had more writing experience than we have.
- the responsibility to keep in mind that everything we write can help us to improve. That means using criticism wisely, not taking it personally, yet considering how it might help us to learn.

Generosity of spirit

Those who belong to a community of writers understand very clearly the effort and the difficulties involved in trying to master the craft. Endeavouring to become a better writer is essentially not about competition and comparison (despite the fact that these are imposed upon schools and probably always will be). One of the most powerful ways that children can help each other to develop is to show 'generosity of spirit'. This might mean offering a sincere compliment to a classmate regarding an entire piece of work or just a well-crafted phrase. It might amount to letting someone know that you appreciate how much effort they've put into their writing. It could take the form of asking a fellow writer for help or for an honest opinion about something you have written. Generosity of spirit has nothing to do with false flattery and is a world away from being envious of other people or being over-inflated about one's own achievements or attainments. It is to do with self-respect as much as respect for others; amounting to a shared appreciation of what hard work writing can be, a willingness to be supportive and to rely on the advice and help of other young writers when needed, and a genuine sense of pleasure in one's own and others' writing successes.

Chapter 2
Dealing with feelings

This chapter presents a variety of techniques for helping children to get the most out of positive and empowering feelings they have while showing them how to modify negative or unpleasant feelings that may inhibit the development of their self-confidence and damage their self-esteem. Although we are concerned with the context of writing and literacy, these techniques have a much broader application, within PSHE programmes for instance and beyond.

Three important points need to be kept in mind which act as a framework for what follows:

- **The mind and the body are linked**. Our thoughts, feelings and physical reactions are connected.

- **We have a conscious part of the mind and a subconscious part**. The conscious part is the self-aware, logical aspect of our thinking that we regard as 'I'. The subconscious part amounts to all of the mental processing that goes on outside our conscious awareness.

- **Our great resources are those of memory and imagination**. We might not be able to recall certain of our experiences at will, but they lie at a subconscious level and still inform our conscious thinking. Imagination is the ability we have to create conscious mental scenarios that need not have any connection with our immediate circumstances. This lies at the heart of our creativity and is an aspect of the core skill of metacognition – our ability to notice, reflect on and manipulate our own thoughts. Metacognition also plays a powerful role in influencing our feelings.

Discussing these points in significant detail goes beyond the scope of this book, though some explanation will be useful in helping you to show children how to become more adept at dealing with their feelings.

The most immediate implication of the points mentioned above is that *through deliberate conscious thought, we can influence the way we feel*. For instance, simply remembering a pleasant experience you had recently will likely bring back the good feelings you enjoyed at the time. You may find yourself smiling and your body posture might change as a result of the thoughts that you chose to recall. You have altered your mental-emotional-physical state through thinking.

The process of deliberately remembering something requires an act of will and a focus of concentration. In other words we choose what memory to have and then we pay attention to it. This is an obvious thing to say of course, but it becomes important when we look at 'catching yourself on' and 'negative self talk'.

Conscious and subconscious

Stated very simply, the conscious part of the mind is like the captain of a ship, while the subconscious is more like the crew. Imagine the captain on the bridge, hands on the wheel, deciding which way to steer the ship. To make those decisions, the captain needs to do certain kinds of thinking – make observations, explore options, judge alternatives, consider reasons, predict possible outcomes, create and refine strategies and reach conclusions.

You'll recognise that these are some of the so-called 'critical' thinking skills, and indeed consciously we are good at doing that kind of critical/analytical, rational and methodical processing.

But the captain is only part of the team. Imagine the subconscious crew getting on with all the tasks it needs to do below decks. The captain has very little idea of the details of the crew's activity but does notice its outcomes.

For instance, and to give a trivial example, I decide to take a sip of coffee. I reach out, bring the mug to my lips, sip the coffee, enjoy the taste, then put the mug back on the coaster. I decided to sip the coffee, but I didn't make decisions about which muscles needed to flex or which joints needed to move, nor did I coordinate the approach of the mug towards my lips. I didn't decide to appreciate the taste of the coffee, while a memory of a conversation I had last week with a friend in a coffee shop came to mind unbidden. All of this highlights an important principle of how the conscious and subconscious interact, which is that *what we consciously think about, we subconsciously react to*. This idea becomes highly relevant as we look at ways of helping children to influence their own thoughts and feelings.

As to the subconscious itself (and again to simplify matters greatly), the thousands of tasks that the crew undertakes break down into three main areas of activity.

1. The subconscious is great at carrying out instructions

These are usually the captain's instructions, sipping coffee being one example of this process. However, if as individuals we are not paying much attention to our conscious thinking, then we might be sending unintentional messages to the crew that influence subconscious behaviour. Again we come back to negative self-talk; the kind of low volume background mental 'muttering' that can so easily occur and that we can so easily miss noticing. When this is going on, we are in effect drip-feeding the reactive subconscious with unhelpful instructions that can 'harden' into negative attitudes and limiting self-beliefs.

The subconscious crew can also be receptive to 'instructions' from other people. Children can be influenced by their peers plus the authority figures of parents, teachers and other adults. The one comment by Ellie's teacher at the start of this book (page 1) had a massively demoralising effect on her and stopped her writing for at least a year. The things that adults say however can have a hugely positive influence. Frank is a friend of mine and deputy head of a school in Essex. He told me that during his early teens he was wasting his time in class and getting into trouble often. The only teacher he got on at all well with was set to retire and during his last week came up to Frank, put his hand on his shoulder and said 'I'm expecting great things of you.' 'I didn't think much about it then,' Frank said, 'but realised that as time went by those few words were affecting me more and more, and for the better.'

I think it's significant that Frank didn't think much about what the teacher said at the time. That is to say, he didn't consciously consider the teacher's words and decide to act on them. But they were being assimilated subconsciously, associated with other ideas at the subconscious level in such a way that they completely turned his attitude around.

2. The subconscious runs the automatic functions of the ship

The complexity of the human body means that consciously we could never make enough decisions to allow us to function. Most of what goes on inside us – physical processes as well as the mental assimilation of sensory data and other information – happens at a subconscious level. An important upshot of this is that a relatively simple and straightforward conscious thought can prompt a huge amount of subconscious activity.

3. The subconscious looks after our memories

During our lives we have millions of experiences, hear and speak countless words, think an untold number of thoughts. Consciously, we forget most of these but subconsciously they are drawn up into a kind of map of what we think the world is like and how we fit into it. In the same way that the captain-and-crew is a handy but simplistic metaphor, so is the notion of a mental 'map'. It's often called the map of reality, but like any map, it is only a representation of the world based on our (conscious and subconscious) interpretation of the things we have experienced and how they have been associated.

The point to make here is that the subconscious is a vast living repository of memories and ideas with a huge potential for creating new concepts and insights. In short, it is a most wonderful resource that we have at our disposal.

Imagination

Imagination is the ability we have to create mental scenarios that need have nothing to do with our immediate circumstances. Our power of imagination brings together the resources of both the conscious and subconscious parts of the mind. That is to say, we can take a memory (drawn from the subconscious 'map') and then deliberately alter it. This becomes important when we look at techniques for modifying memories that generate unpleasant feelings.

The imagination is also the arena where our ideas are created, organised and refined. As such, it 'overlaps' the conscious and subconscious. If as writers we are working on a story for example, we can use our imaginations to deliberately think about a character or what might happen next. But ideas can also pop into mind 'out of the blue', which is to say, they are the outcomes of subconscious assimilation as a result of our conscious intention to think about the story. In that regard, the captain and crew work as a team towards some positive and hopefully pleasurable outcome. A note on conscious intention: to _intend_ to achieve something is not the same as 'trying hard to get there'. Working on a story becomes much more difficult if we sit there and try hard to have ideas – in the same way that trying hard to remember a name makes recollection less likely. In this sense, intention is like the notion of 'will' that we came across in discussing the diamond of success (pages 9–10). It amounts to a clear sense of direction and destination followed by application – this is what I want to achieve, this is how I'll go about it, now I'll knuckle down and have a go.

Inspiration

The imagination shines in the presence of inspiration. As writers, when we are keen to create something new and unique – a story, a poem, an essay. When we are interested in the world around us, when we take pleasure in the effort we make, then we are on the way to what might be called 'self-inspiration'. We fire ourselves up and look forward to the adventure of the writing. That said, other people and their achievements inspire us too; this is fine as long as we bear in mind that being inspired is an active process that has as much to do with what our own actions as with the way we are positively influenced by others.

Many children are keen to ask visiting authors what inspires them, and I have been asked the question numerous times. Before I give any answer myself, I ask the class what they think inspiration means. Their replies include:

- admiring somebody and what they have done
- wanting to be like them
- having ideas
- getting excited about making a story
- wanting to do something (even if you don't know how to do it yet)
- really looking forward to the work
- knowing how to do it
- feeling all glowy, like you're going on an adventure.

I tell children that the word inspiration is a weave of many threads. Its origins are to do with the spirit and the 'breath of god', to blow into and, more recently, to influence or bring alive with an idea or a purpose. So most of what children say relates to classical notions of inspiration. To keep it simple, you might say that being inspired is to do with breathing, but here we breathe in experiences and we breathe out ideas and enthusiasm.

For more on inspiration you can read *A Creative Approach to Teaching Writing* (see Bibliography).

Catch yourself on

This expression (supposedly from Northern Ireland) can mean 'wise up' or 'become aware of yourself'. In the context of dealing with feelings, it applies to the way that unhelpful or negative thoughts can circle around in our minds, like a song in the head that we can't seem to get rid of. When this happens, the subconscious continually reacts to them, perhaps by popping up unwanted memories that reaffirm those thoughts and/or by bringing forward sometimes vague but nevertheless unpleasant feelings. All of this then becomes a vicious cycle which can intensify into a set of limiting self-beliefs and an ongoing negative attitude.

The first step in dealing with this is simply to notice what's happening. This involves not just noticing thoughts but feelings too. While what we might call peripheral or barely noticed thoughts can generate negative feelings, so too can feelings already present create unwanted repetitive thoughts.

As a classroom activity, ask the children to settle themselves and begin paying attention to the thoughts and feelings they're experiencing. It's important to emphasise that children should not distract each other, nor should they try to work out why those thoughts/feelings are coming forward. There's nothing analytical about this; it's simply about noticing.

Top tip

If a child is already upset by something that has happened recently at home or school then they should not take part in this activity. If you allow them to, they will most likely just 'go through it all again' since the event is still fresh and the emotions still raw, and at this stage they probably will not have any strategies for dealing with the memories.

You will probably be able to judge by the children's expressions whether they are remembering good or not so good thoughts. Suggest that if the thoughts are good then they can stay around; if they're bad then please can they fade away. You can use an analogy to help children do this. Maybe the thoughts are like birds and they can fly away now, or perhaps they're like dark clouds but the sun comes out and they simply dissolve. (This is not a frivolous suggestion. Subconscious processing is often highly visual and also symbolic/representational. The subconscious crew will respond effectively to a visual instruction as well as to a verbalised one.)

The catch yourself on activity only needs to last a few minutes, but practise it regularly so that the children become more adept at being self-aware as they learn more and more effective ways of nurturing good thoughts/feelings and modifying bad ones. Conclude the activity by showing the class a beautiful landscape scene, pictures of cute animals, telling a joke or a funny short story. This not only takes their attention away from what they were noticing (especially important if the thoughts were at all negative) but formally ends the session. If you use a picture to round off the activity, ask the children to remember it together with the pleasant reaction they experienced. Afterwards, when they do catch yourself on for themselves, prompt them to remember the picture as a kind of full stop to the game.

The wise observer

This is a very old and effective technique for gaining more control over thoughts and feelings. It means exploiting the full value and potential of pleasant and positive thoughts as well as minimising the effects of negative ones.

Suggest to the class that inside our minds there is a wise observer or 'one who watches wisely'. You can take time beforehand to help children to imagine their own wise observers. Some choose a favourite character from a book, comic or film. Some pick a sporting hero or a TV celebrity. A few children I've met have imagined themselves as being older and wiser. Children might want to draw and write about their wise observers to make the imagined character richer and more vivid later on.

It's also worth looking at what 'wise' and 'wisdom' can mean. The words have their roots in Old English for knowledge, experience, learning and, further back, to the notion of being self-controlled. Wise also has connections with wizard (wysard) meaning a wise man. Note that the idea of learning is different from that of just acquiring knowledge. Learning implies that we have understood something and can apply it in our lives, realise it and make it real in the way we live.

As a classroom activity (having previously practised the catch yourself on technique), ask the children to sit quietly and recall a pleasant memory. It's likely that they will be 'in' the memory, probably as a first person participant. Now ask them to 'step away' from the memory and watch themselves inside it, i.e. from a more detached third person perspective. They can either *be* the one who watches wisely now or be standing just beside him or her (which is a more subtle perspective). The point of the activity at this stage is for children to practise the stepping-away technique, being able to detach themselves from a memory so that they are not so involved.

You can take it further by wondering if anyone watching wisely will notice something new, interesting and pleasant about the memory they're having. This will make it even more enjoyable or fun when they step back in. After a few moments, get the children to go back into the (hopefully enriched) memory and enjoy it even more now.

Run the activity a number of times using pleasant memories. Children can recall the same experiences or choose different pleasant memories each time. When you feel that they are more confident and capable at stepping out/in, show them how to work with memories they don't like and would rather not have.

Ask them to sit quietly and remember an experience they didn't enjoy, emphasising that they can and must choose which memory to work with. As soon as this happens, tell them to step out and become or be with the wise observer. Prompt them to think thoughts like, 'Oh, look at me getting angry over there' or 'Looking at myself, I notice how upset I was'. The point is to get children to practise detaching themselves from negative experiences as they gain a different perspective on the experience they are recalling (in effect they are beginning to recall it in a different way).

It's not about *trying not to* feel angry or upset. The emotions are not being denied or pushed away. There's no effort involved here except the effort of concentration in staying slightly removed from the remembered experience.

You can suggest that looking at the experience in this different way helps the children to learn something new or useful about it – stating it in these vague terms gives children 'creative space' and lots of potential outcomes. If they are the wise observer then this learning will just pop into mind. If they are with the wise observer, then they can say or otherwise express something helpful now.

Again, let me emphasise that this and other techniques may not be suitable for all children: those who have emotional difficulties beyond a lack of confidence and low self-esteem will require more specialised interventions. Also, we're looking at 'dealing with feelings' within the context of confidence issues to do with writing/literacy – although using the imagination in this way does apply to other areas of children's learning.

The danger of generalisations

The philosopher Alfred North Whitehead pinpointed the problem when he said that while we live in detail, we think in generalities. The mental process is a bit like a join-the-dots game, where each dot represents perhaps a real experience or – and I think this is more commonly the case – something we may have misheard or misinterpreted or even one that is imagined. After a few such 'dots' have appeared in the mind, it's easy to join them up according to our pre-existing beliefs and make a picture that might have very little or nothing at all to do with reality.

Generalisations as mental constructs are big, vague and can be hard to shift. They also frequently come with a strong emotional charge that can serve to exacerbate feelings that are already negative and beliefs that are self-limiting. A simplistic example would be if someone criticises a piece of writing I've done. However well intentioned the criticism might be, if my confidence and self-esteem are already low, it's easy for me to take the comments negatively, to feel personally judged, to become upset and to amplify what has been said into a general belief that 'I'll never be any good as a writer'. A further danger is that the generalisation might not express itself as a clear and consciously recognised statement, but rather as a vague (though still strong) feeling of disappointment, anger, resentment, or a sense of being bruised after such an unpleasant verbal attack.

Generalisations are 'big' in the sense that they can loom large in our lives and dominate our perceptions. While the old adage has it that an angry man lives in an angry world, so someone who feels criticised inhabits a world of criticism and is always sensitive to and fearful of being criticised. The literature of NLP (Neuro-linguistic Programming) sums the idea up nicely by saying that 'perception is projection'. The conclusions we have drawn, by whatever means and however misguided, are projected on to our perceptions of the world and then 'feed back' into our minds to strengthen the very beliefs that generated them.

This is not to say that negative or even vindictive criticism doesn't exist – though in a teaching situation it should never be used against children and should be curbed wherever it is found among the children themselves. The point is that 'generalised thinking' is usually unhelpful and inhibits the growth of the individual. As teachers, we can be on the lookout for negative generalisations in the children. These are often expressed by such extremes as *always, never, all, every* and so on. We can help children to deal with them in the following ways.

Ask for evidence

If a child says for example, 'I'm always making mistakes,' gently challenge that by asking them to justify 'always'. If a child shows you a piece of work that contains say ten errors, point out instances in the same piece where no mistakes have been made. Encourage the child to take a different perspective. When I pointed out to one boy that he'd spelt separate as 'seperate' he said sullenly, 'Typical. I've got it all wrong again'. I told him that actually he'd got seven out of the eight letters right.

Another related technique invites the child to look a bit more deeply into where the negative belief might have come from. Use terms such as 'exactly', 'precisely', 'tell me more' etc. 'Where exactly did the belief that you're <u>always</u> doing it wrong come from?' '<u>*Tell me more*</u> about precisely why you think you'll <u>never</u> be any good as a writer?' (Emphasising the 'always' and 'never' creates the opportunity to reconsider them.) In most instances, the child will not be able to supply further information about the generalisation that is holding them back, allowing you to suggest that, 'If you can't gather loads of evidence to support the belief, do you think it might be time to let it go?' (See also Challenging the metaphors on page 26.)

The power of pretend

The writer and philosopher Colin Wilson states that most people live 90% of the time inside their own heads. In other words, our 'realities' are at least as much a construct of our imaginations as of what exists in the wider world 'out there'. If we accept that an angry man lives in an angry world, then imagination has played a significant part in building up and channelling that emotion and projecting it into that man's perception of the outside world.

Imagination is also instrumental in our ability to pretend. By this, and in the context of issues of self-confidence around writing, I'm not suggesting that we tell children they should pretend they are confident. We need to be a bit more subtle and elegant than that. So if a child tells you that they can't do a piece of writing, as a first response you can say, 'Well pretend you can and tell me when you've done it'. Framed in this way, 'pretend' implies that it's only make believe anyway (i.e. not 'real') while 'when' is a *presupposition of success* that may not register on a conscious level but will have a positive influence subconsciously insofar as you feel the child will inevitably carry out the task. ('Make believe' also helps us to 'make beliefs' which, with the right techniques, can be positive and empowering. Again, this is not a question of kidding ourselves but of actively constructing ways of looking at the world and at ourselves that nourish our self-image rather than diminishing it.)

A similar technique, when confronted by a child's limiting belief or perceived inability to carry out a task is to say to the child, 'What would it feel like if you could do it?' or 'Imagine you have already succeeded. What does that feel like and what steps did you take to get there?' Notice the subtle use of the past tense in 'did' which encourages the child to project themselves imaginatively into the future and look back as though they have already succeeded. This is simply another way, among so many, of enabling a child to access those powerful resources of memory and imagination.

Challenging the metaphors

Metaphors are an essential element of our language and in a very profound sense 'frame' our reality (to use one example). Because they are so embedded, it's easy to use them without noticing, nor is it commonly realised that they have such a powerful influence on the way we look at and react to the world. The same can be said of similes, although these tend to be easier to spot.

While metaphors affect a person's general view of life, our primary concern is the link between low self-esteem and writing. (Notice the spatial metaphor 'low' and how easily it goes unrecognised. Notice too how it relates to other similar terms used to talk about negative thoughts and feelings – down, depressed, down in the dumps, weighed down, dragged down, flat, laid low, etc.)

Perhaps the most common writing related metaphor is 'writer's block'. I was once asked by a Year 6 teacher what I, as an author, did about writer's block and what tricks did I use to beat that barrier? I said that I put a door in it and walked through. The children cottoned on immediately and offered plenty of other ways of looking at the phenomenon of not having words or ideas leaping to mind at that particular moment. You could strap on a jet pack and zoom over it, turn into a monster and smash through it, jump to left or right and walk round it, wave a wand and make it disappear… This is not simply some kind of frivolous word game. I suggested to the teacher that if she talked about blocks and barriers, that's how the children would look at them. How about a writer's adventure playground, or a writer's opportunity to think further instead?

The main point to make about negative metaphors is to get into the habit of noticing them when they crop up and either deliberately avoid them in future, or replace them with something more positive and useful.

Redressing the balance

This is the act of finding a positive for every negative that comes along. If a child says they can't do something (even after trying), help them to recall something that they could do, did do and felt a sense of achievement about. Encourage children to develop the habit of 'flipping the mental coin' – as they notice an item of negative self-talk, immediately think the positive opposite. This helps to neutralise the potentially toxic drip-feeding of negative impressions to the reactive subconscious.

Gathering treasures

Allied with the technique of redressing the balance is that of gathering treasures. This amounts to collecting and celebrating occasions when a child has done something well and/or where they have shown what might be called one of the 'noble qualities' of kindness, helpfulness, compassion, empathy and so on. A kind word sincerely meant, or a compliment genuinely offered, is at least as much of an achievement as getting an answer right or scoring well in a test. We can all surely recall things we said and did that helped somebody, solved a problem, cheered them up or gave them a way forward. One school I visited had supplied every child with a notebook that was used as a 'treasures journal', to be used specifically for recalling positive experiences. These included skills-related things like asking a relevant question, justifying an opinion, applying a recently taught rule or technique in a piece of writing, supporting a point of view with reasoned argument and so on.

Changing the memory

When he was about seven years old, Ben had some unpleasant experiences of bullying at the hands of an older boy who lived on the same street and went to Ben's school. After some months, the older boy and his family moved away, though Ben was still plagued by the memories of what he'd suffered.

I found out about this when I did a 'mind warm-up' activity with Ben's class, asking the children to think of a tennis ball then make it float into the air, change colour, turn inside out, morph into a football, a soap bubble etc. As I went through this, I noticed a big grin on Ben's face and asked him about it once the class had settled down to their writing exercise. Ben shrugged and grinned again. 'There was this kid who used to bully me. Whenever I think of him now I make him really small and stamp on him with my shoe. He goes splat and squirts out like tomato ketchup.' Apparently Ben had used the mind warm-up as an opportunity to run through his modified memory of the bully, and gain a degree of satisfaction that had long since taken the place of the fear and humiliation he used to feel.

The trick that Ben had learned is the essence of the memory changing technique. When we recall experiences, we tend to do it in the same way each time. If the memory is a negative one, then bringing it back unchanged simply puts us through the same bad feelings again. But there's no rule to say that we have to do this. Using the power of the imagination, we can deliberately alter the way the memory presents itself in our minds. This changes the locus of control: we're no longer the passive victims of the memory (and the people involved in it) but, rather, the proactive controllers of the contents of the imagery and the feelings associated with it.

The work you've done with the children in showing them how to pay attention to their own thoughts is helpful again now. As a classroom activity, ask the children to recall a *pleasant* experience and to notice as they do so how the memory comes to them…

- Is it in vivid colour, pastels, black and white?
- Can they hear sounds? Just the main sounds or also background sounds?
- If there are voices, notice details of pitch, tone and what is said.
- Are they seeing things through their own eyes (first person perspective) or standing aside looking at themselves in the memory?
- Are things moving? Real time, slow motion or quicker than normal?
- What feelings accompany the memory?
- What else do they notice?

Because this is a good memory, recalling it each time in the way they've noticed preserves it and reinforces its positive and pleasant aspects. You can either leave things as they are or invite the children to have the memory again and this time *enhance* the elements of it that seem significant. If a child recalls in colour, ask them to 'turn up' the colours so that they are more vivid now. Make the sounds clearer. Feel the textures of things and the physical sensations within the memory.

Top tip

If a child says that they can't do it, remember the little linguistic tricks we touched on earlier: say, 'Pretend you can and tell me when you've done it.' If a child says they don't know how to do it say, 'Imagine you've already done it. Look back and see how you did it.' These techniques help to draw out the potential of the child – those which they don't know they have yet. We're working with the imagination here and a child who proclaims that they can't/ don't know how is simply experiencing a failure of imagination (see page 12) which in this case is easy to fix.

When you've run this activity a few times with the class, they'll be ready to deal with less pleasant memories such as being criticised, feeling self-conscious and so on. Again, if any child has been through traumatic rather than simply unpleasant experiences, it is advisable that they do not take part. Also, the memories you want the children to access could be to do specifically with the issue of confidence and self-esteem, and you may want them to relate particularly to writing/literacy.

Explain to the class that they're going to choose a memory of an experience that they haven't enjoyed – but by the power of their imagination they can change things so they'll feel a lot better about it. Tell the children that however they've recalled the memory in the past, now they can change everything about it…

If it's in colour, change the colours round and make them fluorescent and garish. If there are sounds, alter them as you like. Turn the voice of someone who's shouting or taunting into squeaking like Donald Duck. Or if it's a man's voice, change it to a woman's voice or a baby sound like 'ga-ga' coming out of the man's mouth. In other words, the emphasis is on playfulness and fun as children realise that they can change aspects of a memory, which in turn changes their emotional *response* to the memory. That said, Ben introduced an element of cartoon violence into his altered memory of the bully. For him this served as a 'quick anger', a safe emotional release that in his case was helpful. I must admit to doing the same when I work on my own memories, though you may or may not want to suggest it to the class.

Get the children to run through the changes a number of times, 'Until you feel that the memory has really changed. You'll know when that is. *When* you know, look around the room and notice something you haven't noticed ever before, or haven't thought about for a long time'.

This last element of the activity is called a 'break state' – a deliberate break of concentration once the process of change has been completed. It acts like a little full stop in the mind, a signal to the subconscious that the work has been done.

Subsequently, when children either deliberately recall the memory they've worked on (or if it spontaneously pops into mind), it's likely to be remembered in its modified form. If it comes back in its original form, advise the child to go quickly through their set of changes once more. Sometimes the subconscious (which holds the memory in store) needs a little training before it knows what to do.

Finally, there's a small philosophical point to deal with. Sometimes when I talk about changing memories in this way, somebody challenges me – 'Yes but the memory (Ben's bullying etc.) *really happened*. If you change it, you're just fooling yourself.'

Without going into any depth about what 'really' might mean, the point is that in a very significant way, memories are owned by the individual concerned and they can do with them what they like. What we're doing here is endeavouring to modify the unwanted response to unpleasant events that happened in the past – in which case, where are those events now? In a pragmatic sense they're gone; they don't exist except as thought traces in the minds of the people involved.

Another point to consider is that the mind doesn't record experiences like a camera. Our perceptions are subjective; we interpret the world. Our entire subconscious map of 'reality' is a rich and complex network of associations and interpretations. Thinking back, I recall a time when as a teenager I was walking in town and some girls were laughing at me… Or were they really laughing at me, or at something else? Since I am the 'owner' of that memory, I can choose to believe they were really laughing at me or that they weren't. If I decide that they were laughing at me, and if I have a way of changing the memory so I don't feel foolish or humiliated as I recall it, what's wrong with that? Besides, I don't know what really happened but I know that I can have the changed memory now and I needn't any longer feel bad about it.

Quick change trick

This technique allows you to work on feelings without the need to recall any memories to which they are attached. In fact, the technique can be effective even if you *don't know* what memories have caused them, or if the feelings are the result of a whole cluster of past experiences.

This activity works best as a one-to-one session. So let's suppose you were working with Tony who wanted to do something about his feeling of low self-confidence.

You: If the feeling you want to change had a shape, what would it be?

Notice how Tony's point of attention is on the 'shape' of the feeling and not any memories associated with it.

Tony: It's round.

Y: How big is it?

T: About half the size of a football.

Y: What colour is it?

T: Greyish green.

Y: How does it weigh?

T: Heavy.

Y: Describe its texture.

T: Kind of knobbly like an orange.

Y: Squeeze the shape. What happens?

T: It squeezes ever so slightly, but you can't squash it out of shape.

Y: Pretend you can scratch it with a blade…

T: It leaves a dull streak. Underneath it's greyer, less green.

Y: Pretend it has a smell…

T: Kind of sour.

Y: Imagine you can tap it with a spoon and it makes a sound.

T: A dull clunk.

Y: Where inside you do you feel it?

T: In my stomach.

Top tip

Most people 'mould' the feeling with their hands as they talk about it. That's to be encouraged as it gives them another way of making the changes.

Once you've come this far, tell Tony that he's going to change everything about the feeling. Tell him you'll mention each part of it again, but you'll do it quickly so he has to work quickly. Explain that he doesn't have to think about the changes but can use the first thing that comes into his mind.

You: Change the shape now.

Tony: It's more floppy now, like a big soap bubble.

Y: Change the colour.

T: It's gone clear. I keep getting the soap bubble. There's like rainbow colours in it now.

Y: Weight?

T: It hasn't got any weight, it's floaty.

Y: What does it feel like?

T: It's like thin rubber. I can squeeze it and it doesn't burst.

Y: Can you scratch it?

T: I don't want to burst it yet…

Y: Smell?

T: A fresh, clean smell.

Y: Sound?

T: A bit squeaky when I move my hand over it.

Y: Put the feeling somewhere else.

T: It's on the end of my nose.

Y: What do you want to happen to it now, so you know you've finished?

T: It floats away all by itself.

Y: Now look out of the window –

This last instruction is the 'break state' that we met on page 29.

Y: Now imagine the new shape again and notice how the feeling has changed.

It's likely that the child will tell you that the bad feeling isn't so strong now, or even that it's gone away (which is great). Tell them to keep the new feeling in a safe place in their thoughts. Conclude the activity by saying that they can now think about the new shape whenever they want, and must certainly imagine it if any trace of the old feeling comes back.

Take it further: Multisensory thinking

Think about the word 'soft' for example; it can be a word linked with sound or with texture. Similarly, the word 'bitter' can refer to a taste or an emotion. There are many terms in the English language that overlap the senses, an idea that children understand tacitly from an early age – for instance the connection between colour and mood; being red with rage, white with fear, green with envy, yellow with cowardice. Some of these probably hark back to our physiology. When we are enraged we literally flush, when frightened or shocked the blood drains from our faces and we turn pale. Other explanations are more obscure. One possible explanation of the green-envy link goes back to the old belief in the four 'humours' that gave rise to various physical conditions. It was once thought that jealousy created an excess of bile in the body that imparted a pale greenish tinge to the skin.

Fascinating as these ideas are, the 'multisensory' nature of some words offers another practical tool that can help us to modify our feelings. Clearly we absorb sensory impressions through all of our senses. Subsequently, when we represent our understanding of the world in our imaginations – through memories and new mental constructions – many people develop the habit of relying more on one sensory mode than another. This insight is an important feature of the educational movement known as 'Accelerated Learning' first popularised by Colin Rose in a book of that name which appeared in the mid-1980s.

Thus some people rely more on visual imagery when they imagine things: they are easily able to look at a black and white picture and imagine it in colour. Similarly their memories are more likely to be highly visual, in colour and with plenty of visual detail. Other people are more familiar and comfortable with imagining sounds – they are more 'auditorily-oriented' thinkers. The sound elements of a memory are likely to be more prominent for them, while visuals might be less clear and colours dulled or even absent. Some individuals are more tactile (kinaesthetic) in their thinking. They may be more connected to their bodies in that when they remember the accompanying physical sensations are relatively powerful. (The word 'remember' can be read as re-member, which means to 'bring back into the members'; to recreate in the flesh the physical sensations that were present when an event first happened. Some people are much more physical 're-memberers' than others.) Such people may also use body language more overtly when talking about what they are thinking. (Sometimes more tactile thinkers will 'mime' their thoughts even if they are not speaking them out.)

The upshot of this insight is to identify the main sensory component(s) of a memory and to cross-match it with other senses. So if a child remembers being spoken to harshly, flag up the idea that harsh can refer to a sound or a texture. If the child's memory of 'harsh' is predominantly auditory, you could ask, 'If you could touch that sound, what does it feel like?'. The child may say rough – which still maintains the link with someone's voice – or he might say 'A bit knobbly'. Asking the child then to 'smooth out' the texture in his imagination means that you helped the child to step away from the auditory quality of the harshness in his unpleasant memory while going through the process of modification we looked at in the quick change technique (page 30).

Playing with the idea that sensory impressions can be cross-matched not only offers a mental tool for gaining more control over one's feelings, but offers a way for children to enrich their use of language – see the activity 'What are you thinking?' on page 44.

Using unpleasant feelings positively

Consider inadvertently putting your hand on a hot radiator. Within a moment you feel the pain and snatch your hand away. The pain is unpleasant, but it has served two positive purposes – to remove your hand from the heat quickly to minimise the damage, and to teach you to be more careful next time when near hot surfaces.

This is a common and simple example of what we might call the 'principle of positive purposes'. In this case (and we could think of many more), the pain response is essentially a *protective* impulse. We could not help but snatch our hand away; it is an automatic, subconsciously generated reaction. We might say that the crew is protecting the captain from further suffering, while offering the admonition to pay more attention.

Similarly, even unpleasant emotions can be regarded as positive resources, if we are prepared to make that leap of the imagination and look at them and then use them in that way. Ben's anger and fear when he was bullied for example (page 27) could be carrying some potentially useful messages. The fear could be thought of as telling Ben that at the moment he is relatively weak and vulnerable. The anger reflects his high ethical standards over the 'wrongness' of the bully's actions. These may be obvious insights to Ben or ideas that he might not consciously consider (and so cannot positively utilise) unless encouraged to do so.

The root of the word emotion is based on the Latin 'emovere', from e- (variant of ex-) 'out' + movere 'move', to move out or away. Looked at in this way an emotion is usually an urge to move, *to do something about the situation*. So as a general strategy, when we experience an unpleasant emotion, we might ask ourselves two key questions:

- What positive message does this feeling carry?
- What can I do to change the situation?

Thinking again about Ellie (page 1), the teacher's comment filled her with a sense of despondency and disillusionment. In thinking about what 'positive message' those emotions might carry, we could take a look at where the words come from.

> *Despondency: from Latin dēspondēre 'to promise, make over to, yield, lose heart'; from de- + spondēre to promise.*

There are useful pickings in these etymological morsels. Promise, for instance, means 'a declaration that something will or will not be done, given etc.'. For this aspect of despondency to have any meaning, Ellie (once she has begun to reason things through in this way) must make a self-promise (her teacher certainly didn't promise anything by her comment). She can promise either to 'yield' to her teacher's words and decide not to write any more, or she can promise to continue writing because the strength of her feeling *tells her how precious her writing is to her* (and to prove her misguided teacher wrong!).

The notion of despondency, meaning to 'lose heart', is interesting too. Classically, the heart is the seat of the emotions (the urge to move). To lose heart then suggests that Ellie has no will to move, presumably away from her present state of feeling disinclined to write. And yet the feeling remains with her. It is still trying to tell her something beyond the (presumably initial) discouragement she experienced. The fact that the emotion is ongoing means that her 'heart' is still engaged with the issue: the message is still coming through to do something about it. This also highlights the important point that an emotion is not a 'state' (something static and unmoving) but a process. Regarded in this way, we might say that Ellie is not in a state of despondency but, because the emotion is ongoing, is 'doing despondency' brilliantly. The message to move is loud, clear – and repeated.

This idea features prominently in the eclectic bag of techniques known as Neuro-linguistic Programming (NLP), which explores the relationships between a person's neurology, the use of language and how it can be applied to modify unhelpful thoughts and feelings, moving an individual towards a fulfilment of potential.

In this context, I am also reminded of Buckminster Fuller, American neo-futuristic architect, systems theorist, author, designer and inventor, who once said 'I seem to be a verb'. (The full quote is, 'I live on Earth at present, and I don't know what I am. I know that I am not a category. I am not a thing – a noun. I seem to be a verb, an evolutionary process – an integral function of the universe'.) For me this is not grandiose rhetoric but a soaring vision of what someone can aim to achieve.

> *Disillusionment: being freed from illusion or conviction; disenchantment.*

This word, disillusionment, is a rich playing field of ideas for those interested in language (as Ellie is). Illusion itself comes from the Latin to mean 'to mock at'. I'm not sure that Ellie was mocking herself or fooling herself in showing that she loved writing. Her idealism lay in her desire to improve as a writer, not in any false assessment that the work she handed in was brilliant or the best she could ever achieve. Oddly then, for her teacher to *dis*illusion Ellie means (linguistically) that she was removing any sense of self-mockery, had it existed, and was certainly not herself mocking Ellie.

In terms of 'conviction', what was Ellie convinced of? Perhaps that her teacher would be interested in her work and offer some sound and supportive advice. The fact that this didn't happen might shake Ellie's conviction in her teacher's opinion but, since the opinion was so ill-considered and unsupported by reasons (apart from pointing out technical errors), surely not in the work itself or the enjoyment Ellie had in writing it?

The root of enchantment lies in the Latin *incantare* meaning 'to sing' (akin to 'chant') and has connections with the Greek term for 'voice'. In a more familiar sense, enchantment means magic and fascination. When we write, we 'sing' our thoughts and feelings, we search for and find our voice. We recognise magic and fascination (something going beyond the normal and everyday) in the ideas that pour through the mind and then flow out on to the page. The greatest cruelty involved in disenchantment is to dampen the fascination a young writer feels for words and ideas. And again, the fact that Ellie's feeling was still with her suggests to me that she was looking for a way to re-enchant the world of her writing.

You might argue that Ellie was 'wallowing' in the negative emotions generated by her teacher's comment. But what does that mean? Ordinarily we interpret the idea as someone knowingly indulging themselves by hanging on to those feelings for reasons they may or may not be consciously aware of; wanting sympathy perhaps or, in this case, as an excuse not to write – 'I can't bring myself to put pen to paper because my teacher made me feel so bad about myself'. Having met Ellie, I doubt that's true. In any event, if we are, as Buckminster Fuller said, 'verbs not nouns', that means the unpleasant feelings are still trying to move us in another direction and in my experience usually a positive one. Unpleasant emotions that linger often (I won't say always) seek to serve the principle of positive purposes. If we carry with us the intention that this is so then the chances are that negative emotions will strengthen us and move us in a positive direction.

The above might be called the analytical approach to exploring and changing feelings (though not in the conventional sense of a psycho-analytical process). I've written about it at length because delving into the origins of the words that lie behind our feelings can yield a rich seedbed of insights, which in turn can supply us with information and strategies to change the way we feel.

The process can be much simpler. Once a child's perspective shifts, their emotions can shift. During one workshop I ran, a boy came up to me after I'd set the class a writing task and told me that he couldn't do it. When I asked him why he said, 'Because I'm thick.' Off-the-cuff I replied, 'Well pretend you're thin and show me when you've done it.' He laughed, went away and finished the task. My almost frivolous comment had tilted the word 'thick' to a new angle, caused him some amusement (modified his response to it) and offered a strategy for progress. Similarly, when working with another class, as we were discussing metaphors we decided that we would no longer call it writer's 'block' but writer's 'adventure playground' (see page 24). The shift of perception gave many of the children access to different and more positive feelings when experiencing the admittedly frustrating situation of not having a flow of ideas or words at the forefront of our minds at that moment.

Yet another easy strategy is to bypass any analysis at all and simply, stubbornly, dig your heels in and decide to do what you want and love to do. This is sometimes called 'the law of reverse effect' and again depends upon the young writer making up their own mind. The attitude is supported by an effective mental technique called 'flipping the coin'.

Flipping the coin

This is a version of the catch yourself on idea. The notion is to become aware of negative thoughts and 'flip the coin' to deliberately think of the positive opposite. So in light of the comment made to Ellie, she could flip the mental coin and turn despondency into 'respondency' and disenchantment into re-enchantment. By the same token (no pun intended, though I'm glad I thought of it), if the comment made to Ellie created a mental image – let's say of her throwing her writing book and pen away – then flipping the coin would generate a new image of her retrieving the book and pen and putting them in a safe place. (The coin metaphor is useful because it suggests that all of us always have the capacity to experience both positive and negative emotions. The comparison fails perhaps in speaking of 'flipping' the coin. Perhaps a more empowering but clumsier title for the technique would be 'deliberately turning the coin positive side up.')

To work directly on feelings, with some practise it's possible to turn a feeling into an abstract shape/object (as in the quick change activity) and then flip the coin so that all aspects of it transform into a positive opposite. In other words, the quick change happens all-at-once in a moment, with more positive feelings arriving just afterwards.

Again, let me emphasise that these are not frivolous 'mind games'. Our sense of reality and identity are rooted in our thoughts and feelings which are consolidated into a network of beliefs that create our underlying attitude to life – that is, how we 'stand' and 'orient ourselves' in the world. These are *our* thoughts and *our* feelings which, when they are unpleasant, unwanted and unhelpful to us, though they may have been 'put there' by other people they are now in our inner domain and we have the right to use them as we will. As the old saying goes, we see the world not as it is but as we are. This book is all about ways of making positive changes to who we are.

I might add in passing that adult authors often go through the same issues of bruised confidence and lowered self-esteem that can be (albeit inadvertently) influenced by others. Writers aspiring to be published need to deal with the frustration of waiting often months for a response from a publisher or literary agent, the disappointment of repeated rejections of their work and then, when the book is published, possible low sales and adverse comments from the critics.

So it is that resilience is as important a quality in adults as it is in young writers. That resiliency is made all the more robust by a deep-rooted love of the craft and of language itself.

Literacy link

Flipping the coin is also a good way of generating ideas for stories.

Be your own good friend

A negative self-image can be very damaging, especially when it develops as the result of cultural influences, what's fashionable, what celebrities look like, peer pressure etc. In that sense it is not truly a *self*-image but one determined by others.

Undoubtedly it's difficult for some children to remain aloof if they're unhappy about their body image and what they think others say about them. At the same time, on the brink of adulthood, young people are searching for a sense of identity; for a way of finding out who they are and what their purpose is in the world. (With that in mind, working on one's writing is a *great* way of exploring oneself, the world and finding an individual voice.)

That said, it does not take a great deal of effort to do some reflecting with the intention of achieving a sense of balance. Suggest these techniques to the children:

- **Positive self review**. Take a few minutes to think back to the times when you have done something kind, compassionate or generous. What have you done in a confident way? When have you shown determination? Remember times when effort brought success and how good that sense of achievement felt. Think back to any occasions when, even if you made a mistake or did something you regretted, you took responsibility for your actions and tried to put things right.

- **Recall too when other people made positive comments about you**. Think of those who are truly your friends and the good times you've had together.

- **Consider what you can do to further improve the way you feel about yourself**. Thank someone for a small kindness. Show a sincere interest in what someone is saying – or ask a question about something they're interested in. We're all familiar with the idea of taking an interest in something; it might be more accurate to say that here you're *giving* an interest.

- **If someone says something negative about you, consider that the comment might be saying more about them than about you**. If someone tries to make you feel small it could well be because they want to make themselves feel bigger (at your expense, if you're willing to pay out).

A handy little technique is called the *mental mirror*. All you need to do is imagine that you are protected by a mental mirror. Whenever anybody makes a negative comment about you, it never reaches you but just bounces away harmlessly. It may even reflect back on the person who made it, based on the principle that 'we reap what we sow'.

- **Sometimes criticism is constructive and not intended to hurt**. Be wise enough to tell the difference between that which is useful to you and petty sniping comments.

- **Another powerful technique is to sift out any aspects of yourself that you wouldn't like if you saw them in somebody else**. If you don't like other people to say petty things about others, then if you spot that in yourself, decide to put a stop to it.

- **Someone once said, 'It's not what you look like that matters. It's the animating spirit that counts'**. What qualities and values lie deep inside you that, when they show themselves, make you the unique person you are, and which create the vision of your future?

Quiet, personal minutes of reflection like this are all about self-respect, the act of looking back again to gain a clearer view of who we truly are. As Oscar Wilde said, 'Be yourself, everyone else is already taken'.

Top tip
Most of these ideas can be applied specifically to the context of writing. This might in fact be the most effective way of introducing children to the notion of an honest, balanced review of themselves. Ask children to look back at a piece of their work and review it in the light of those points above which most readily apply.

As someone once said…

Quotes have been described as 'little gems that reflect the world's wisdom' (writer Ben Leech). They also often say in a few words what we might have been feeling but couldn't find the language to express. A powerful quote will clarify our thoughts and give an emotional boost to buoy us up through the day.

Here are some quotes that mean something special to me. Invite the children to find others that appeal to them. Pick a quote at random and spend a few minutes discussing it with the class as a way of warming up for any lesson or for a writing session.

'Learn from the mistakes of others. You can't live long enough to make them all yourself.' – Eleanor Roosevelt.

'God made the writer, then took some scraps that were left and made three critics.' – Attributed to various sources.

'How much easier it is to be critical than to be correct.' – Benjamin Disraeli.

'A writer is a person for whom writing is more difficult than it is for other people.' – Thomas Mann.

'The most effective way to do it, is to do it.' – Amelia Earhart.

'Writing is like breathing. I do it to be alive.' – Douglas Hill, children's author.

'To avoid criticism do nothing, say nothing, be nothing.' – Elbert Hubbard.

'Out of clutter, find simplicity. From discord, find harmony. In the middle of difficulty, find opportunity.' – Albert Einstein.

'When some points at the moon, the fool looks at the finger but the wise one looks at the moon.' – Traditional Chinese saying.

'Even if you're on the right track, you'll get run over if you just sit there.' – Will Rogers.

'We struggle not to win or lose, but to keep something alive.' – T. S. Eliot.

Story stone

The intention of this section has been to show children how to use their imaginations to boost positive thoughts/feelings and to change unhelpful and negative ones. The same skills that they have been developing here will be equally useful when they come to do their thinking time and the writing that follows.

A useful technique is called *anchoring*. This is a link that is created between a particular positive behaviour and something that is under our conscious control, such as a small pebble. In other words, the behaviour is 'anchored' or held in place by the pebble.

To apply the idea, invite each child in the class to bring in a small pebble that they like and that they have chosen to link with feeling good about themselves, having lots of useful ideas, feeling a sense of achievement at a piece of work well done etc. As you practise the various techniques described in this book, encourage the children to hold their story stones and in their imaginations to feel some of that positive energy going into the stone.

Like any technique, this needs to be practised regularly. When the object-behaviour link has been established, it can work both ways: when a child *wants* to have ideas, feel confident etc., they pick up the stone and this acts as a subconscious trigger for the behaviour or outcome they are looking for.

One teacher who heard about the story stone didn't like the idea because she thought it was a kind of conditioning. But this is not the case because each child *chooses* when to hold the stone to reconnect with the desired behaviour. In other words, the child has control over positive behaviour as a way of overcoming negative behaviour that previously was not under their control – like a fear of the blank page, anxiety about 'getting it wrong', worrying about negative criticism and so on.

Another teacher was concerned in case a child lost their story stone. 'I know several children in my class who would be very upset if they lost their stone!' We decided that a good solution would be to have a *whole-class story stone*. This is a larger pebble that the teacher keeps on their desk. When the children first bring their story stones to class they touch them to the class stone and repeat this action as their own story stones accumulate positive energy (i.e. as the object-behaviour anchor is established). Thus the class stone becomes a powerful repository of positive associations. If a child loses their personal story stone, you need only explain that they can choose another pebble and, by touching it against the class stone, make it as powerful as the original one.

(Incidentally, the same teacher then became worried about losing the class story stone. I said, just slightly tongue in cheek, 'Then you get a damn great boulder and put it in the hall. This becomes the whole school story stone.')

The story stone idea is not as off-the-wall as you might think. Many professional writers use little rituals and routines to get themselves in the mood to write, to switch on the create flow. Just type 'writing rituals' into your search engine to access lots of examples – some of them much more weird and wonderful than story stones!

Chapter 3
Writing games

Some children struggle to have ideas for things to write about in the first place and this can be a great knockback to confidence in their own ability. One of the underpinning presuppositions of this book is that young writers will be more prepared to engage with the technicalities of writing when they know what it is that they want to say and have ways of generating, organising and refining their ideas. Once the context exists, the rules make more sense. In short, when they know how to create a route map, they know they have somewhere to go.

There are many books on having ideas for writing and some are listed in the Bibliography. Meanwhile, here are a few tried and tested techniques for kickstarting the process. While most of these focus on narrative prose, the thinking and writing skills that the children pick up, not to mention their increased confidence, apply equally to non-fictional forms of writing.

Coin flip

Not to be confused with flipping the coin on page 35, this simple technique allows children to create ideas from virtually nothing and then develop them systematically. Begin with a picture or just a sentence and invite children to ask yes-no questions to accumulate information.

> *'Kenzie hurried down the street, turned left at the corner and immediately hid in the nearest shop doorway.'*

A sentence like this suggests a scenario, an image that children can visualise, thus giving them a direction for their questioning straight away. Yet it is sufficiently vague to tempt the children to want to find out more – an intriguing mystery to be investigated. For pictures to use as inspiration in this activity, see **Bloomsbury Online Resource 3A**.

When instructing children on the coin flip game, bear the following in mind:

- There's no need to write out the questions. If the answer to a question is no (tails), then usually there's no need to write anything. This makes the activity more attractive to children who 'don't like writing'.

- When the answer to a question is yes (heads), there's no need to write it out as a whole sentence – a simple note will do.

- Once an answer has been obtained, children can't alter it. No matter how much they want an answer to be yes for instance, if the coin indicates no then that's final (but see the point on refining ideas).

- However, it is possible to modify an idea to obtain the answer you want. If a child asks, 'Is it raining?' and the answer is no, if rain is important in the story the child can have another bite of the apple by asking, 'Is it going to rain soon?'. With a little ingenuity the answer the child wants will be obtained.

- Questions must be relevant, sensible and consistent with questions that have been previously asked; an important benefit of the technique is that children are required to assimilate an increasing amount of information as the narrative unfolds.

Sometimes a child will ask an apparently nonsensical question – 'Is the man in the car a Martian?' – which has no bearing on previously asked questions or on the logical consistency of the story. When this situation crops up, point out that everything in the story must be there for a reason that makes sense within the narrative and that helps the story to be the best it can be. So in this case you can ask, 'If the answer was yes, how the man being a Martian helps the story to make sense?'. Because the child has probably just snatched the Martian idea out of the blue, he will now try and create some logical reason for it, rather than having thought it through before. Such logic will be shaky as the child tries to think 'on the run'. 'He's a Martian because he wants to invade the world.' Keep pressing for reasons. 'But why does he want to invade the world?' 'Because he's evil.' 'But why does the fact that he's evil want to make him take over the world, and how does his plan involve driving around in a car?'

The point here is not to show the child that they have had a 'bad' idea but to highlight that more thoughtful questions, and ones which fit in with what is already known, help the story to grow more 'organically'. Your persistent questioning demonstrates that 'first snatched thoughts' do not usually help a child to build a robust logical consistency in the narrative.

- Show children how to translate open questions into closed ones. For instance, suggesting that a child investigates *who* is in the story opens the doorway to many questions about the characters: asking *where* the story takes place similarly generates abundant questions about setting. Putting the big open questions up on the board before a coin flip session – *where, when, what, who, how, why* – will act as a constant prompt for further questioning.

- Prompt and guide rather than supply children with particular closed questions – that's doing the work for them. Prompting with an open question usually achieves this. Similarly you might say, 'You mentioned Kenzie earlier. I'd be interested to know four things about what she looks like.'

- Children always have the option *not* to flip the coin. Sometimes a child will come up with a really good idea. When this happens, suggest to them that rather than 'gamble' by asking a question, they simply use the idea in the story. This option gives children a sense of control. Besides, one of the aims of the coin flip game is to wean children off it, to develop their confidence in making up their own minds.

- Often playing the game leads to frustration. A child might have wanted a 'yes' answer but got a 'no' instead, or vice versa. Remind children that they have to stick with the answers they're given. However, after they have accumulated a certain number of answers, pause the activity and say, 'Have a look at the information you've got. If there is anything that you would change, for reasons you've thought about, that would make it a better story, now you can make those changes.' It's useful to follow this with a feedback session where children have the option to mention a couple of things that they've changed and why.

The coin flip technique helps children to build stories from scratch. It also works when a child gets stuck in the middle of a piece of writing. I always allow the option for a child in this position to pause and ask some yes-no questions. This will usually get them out of the rut. Interestingly, 'no' responses – when the child wanted 'yes' – are also useful insofar as they demonstrate that the child *already knew their own mind*. In this case, the child can go with the 'yes' option, especially if (as is usually the case) they can tell you why they wanted the answer to be yes in the first place.

Narrative line

The coin flip technique works well in conjunction with the narrative line visual planner.

FIG 3.1   Narrative line

Most children know that a story has a beginning, a middle and an end. I explain to them that's what it looks like when it's finished. During the thinking/planning stage, ideas can pop into mind from any part of the story (because subconsciously we are already assimilating the entire narrative). We can also consciously focus on a particular part of the story: I might have an idea for the dramatic ending before I have much of an inkling of what happens in the middle for instance.

A narrative line organiser accommodates the way that the imagination works, allowing us to have ideas in any order, while offering a means of organising them along the way. As with the coin flip technique, the narrative line allows stories to grow from almost nothing. I might decide that to make my story more interesting, I'd like some 'danger' around the middle of the tale. I simply indicate that on the line and then use the coin flip to find out more and/or just add notes as ideas come to mind.

A variation of the idea is to write thoughts down in scraps of paper, which can then be arranged along the line as the planning of the story proceeds. Ideas that children are pretty sure they'll want to use are placed above the line, while ideas that require more thought, and which may be discarded, are placed below. The less sure a child is about any particular idea, the further below the line it is placed. One benefit of using 'story scraps' in this way is that they can easily be rearranged as required.

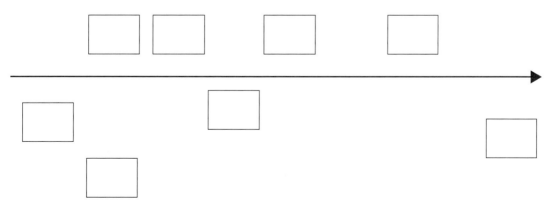

FIG 3.2   Narrative line with story scraps

Plot seeds

Plot seeds consist of a few sentences which outline the plot of a story that children can then develop, individually or working as a team; through discussion/decision or by introducing the random factor of the coin flip. More ambitiously, children can use a plot seed as the basis for making a story grid (pages 51–52), using pictures and/or words that bring together motifs, constituent features that you would commonly find in a story of that kind. Plot seeds can also be used as starter ideas for minisagas (page 61): children can either attempt a minisaga for themselves, or you can prepare them beforehand – writing over the word count or under it – for children to edit.

Here are some ideas you might want to use (age of target audience is in brackets):

- **Monster run**. Neil and Steve spend the evening watching scary movies. When it's time for Steve to go home, Neil warns Steve to be careful of the monsters who will chase him on the way. What does Steve think and do on his way home? (11–13)

- **The Search**. Thomas Karnak searches for his missing brother Karl in the endless forests of Eastern Europe. Karl Karnak set out three years ago to find the legendary castle of the evil Baron Nocta, and nothing has been heard of him since. (11–13)

- **But Mum, there's a monster upstairs!** Tony Stern wants to stay up and watch TV but his parents insist that he goes up to bed. Tony comes back down a few minutes later complaining that there's a monster in his room. Each time Mr and Mrs Stern send their son back, he returns with a more outrageous claim. (5–7) (See the full story on pages 95–98.)

- **Barry**. Kevin Clarke's family, who are colonists on Mars, agree to host the Bradburys who are about to embark on the Star Rider project, a one-way journey to a nearby star. Barry Bradbury is the same age as Kevin Clarke. At first the boys are cautious of one another but soon become friends – though when Kevin learns of Barry's shocking secret the foundations of their friendship are shaken. (11–13)

- **Lost in the fog**. Tim and Tina Taylor the time travelling twins find Eleanor Bradley wandering list in a 'time mist' and help her to find her way home. (7–10)

- **Out on a limb**. Anna Williams wants to join the Double Darers. Nigel Lloyd doesn't want a girl in the group and tries to put her off by insisting she takes a 'bravery test'. (10–12)

Note: These stories are part of a guided reading pack published by Thinking Child (www.thinkingchild.org.uk). For more examples of plot seeds, see **Bloomsbury Online Resource 3B**.

Top tip
Story seeds can be taken from previously published tales, or children can create their own to swap and share based on stories they have written.

Heads and tails

Clip a few paragraphs out of a story to show to the class and ask children to decide what led up to that point and what might happen next. Children don't have to write the entire story (though you might want them to try based on time available). The emphasis of the activity is on developing creativity and inferential thinking.

Here are a few to try out, based on some of the plot seeds on page 42:

1. The strange fog whirled and danced around them like a pale ballet dancer. Then something touched Tina's face and she let out a little squeak of fear. Then something touched Tim's hand and he jumped with shock.

So – you *are* real! The unknown voice spoke again. And slowly a misty shadow appeared before the children. It came towards them, closer, closer… Until they could see that it was a little girl, no older than themselves.

Tim was still unsure about what was happening, but Tina decided the best course of action was to be friendly. She held out her hand.

"Hello. I'm Tina Taylor and this is my brother Tim."

"Pleased to meet you I'm sure. My name is Eleanor Bradley. But you may call me Ellie."

"We're pleased to meet you too Ellie. But what are you doing wandering about in the Tulgey Woods all by yourself?'"

As Tina spoke she noticed how Ellie was dressed; in a very old-fashioned way with a black short-sleeved dress that had been patched and mended many times. She also had on a lacy shawl and wore boots that were laced up to above her ankles.

"Where have you come from Ellie?" Tina wanted to know, although she had a feeling that she already knew.

"Well from Kenniston of course."

Tina smiled. "Perhaps I should have said *when* have you come from?"

"In other words," said Tim, "what year do you think this is?"

Ellie looked puzzled for a moment and then said, "Why, 1895 of course."

The twins looked at one another. "I think she's got lost in a time fog," Tina said.

"Poor thing."

(from "Lost in the Fog")

2. I stepped up to the huge gaping entranceway to Nocta's castle and looked back at the early summer sunshine flickering down through the trees. My earlier suspicions and the fears that followed them seemed melodramatic now, and I felt rather foolish at the thought of confronting Nocta's minions, should they in fact exist…

Perhaps they did not, for after three hours of diligent searching I had found no one. The place was empty, left as it had been at the time of Nocta's death. But the mystery of the letters and Adam's absence still remained. The day was drawing on now and the sky was darkening towards evening. I had only the cellars left to search.

Please do not misunderstand me. I am no coward – at least that is my own considered opinion. Nor do I regard myself as squeamish. Yet what I saw in the first of the cellars brought a scream tearing up from my throat; the urge to run headlong away from the horror was upon me and took all of my will to control.

The four…shapes…upon the stone slabs had once been living, breathing people. Now they more closely resembled the dried husks of flies trapped and fed upon in the spider's lair.

In the first few moments I had noticed the gold ring on the finger of one of those victims, but it took me many minutes to gather the courage to look at it in detail and confirm the worst of my fears.

(from 'The Search')

3. Barry was about to say something else. But then he stared past me and was gone from sight, before I could blink.

'Barry! What –'

'No. NO!' He yelled. I caught sight of him like a flash of colour in the green gloom.

A red light came on above the airlock door as he reached it and smashed his fist hard into it, denting the metal.

Then it registered in my head. A red emergency light.

At first you could hardly feel the loss of air pressure: just a tickling in the lungs, a faint popping of the ears. The fronds and tall leaves around me stirred in a breeze that would grow to a storm and then to silence as the atmosphere in the chamber gushed out. Finally, it would be impossible to breathe. Impossible to live. I wondered if it would be a painful way to die, and a bright white panic caught light in my chest and began burning through my body.

(from 'Barry')

What are you thinking?

Helping children to notice their own thoughts in the context of dealing with feelings also improves their ability to notice details in their mind's eye prior to writing. Take a sentence like:

'Only one box was opened on the table. Bowman smiled at the visitor.'

It's vague so we don't learn much. However, it's likely that many children will have 'filled in the dots' and created a richer imagined scenario than the information in the sentence itself supplies.

Having read or shown the sentence to the class, ask children to notice what they imagined and jot down their ideas (without telling classmates). Then collect ideas. Distinguish between ideas that have been inferred from the sentence itself and those that have just been 'made up'. For instance:

- Because a table is mentioned, it's more likely to be indoors.

- The other character mentioned is a visitor, so perhaps this is where Bowman lives.

- 'Only one box' creates the impression that there were other boxes on the table, but that only this one was open. (The phrase is ambiguous however and could indicate that there was just one box on the table, and that it was opened.)

Practising this kind of inferential thinking develops children's analytical/reasoning abilities when reading text. Collecting the ideas that are more speculative allows you to value the children's thinking: the fact that Bita imagined a small modern-style room and Jaydon imagined a large old-fashioned room is fine. If they were working together to produce a piece of writing, each child could argue the case for using their ideas, in terms of which scenario works best in the context of the story.

Using the ideas collected, revisit the section on multisensory thinking (page 31) to help children enrich their imagined scenarios even more.

- Imagine that Bowman speaks. What does his voice sound like?
- Notice two (or more) interesting details about the visitor.
- Take time to look slowly around the room and notice further details of colour, décor etc.
- Take a deep breath. There is an aroma in the room, what is it?

And so on. Develop concentration further by taking the children on a tour of the surrounding area. Imagine the room is a study in Bowman's large house. Either ask the children simply to 'wander around the house and collect some more observations', or guide them with prompt sentences.

'Turn and face the door to the study. Beside the door is a small round table with a sculpture on it. Note a few details of the sculpture. Open the study door. Ahead of you is a long hallway. The floor is made of large black-and-white tiles in a checkerboard pattern. Ahead and to the left is a flight of stairs: you would need to walk towards the front door which is about 15 paces ahead of you to reach the bottom of the stairs. However, ten steps in front of you to the right is a door to another room. Walk those ten paces, open the door on the right – noticing the shape and colour of the door handle and what it is made of – and step into the room.'

Offering the children increasingly longer and more involved 'imaginary journeys' develops their ability to concentrate, notice and remember details. Most if not all of the children will reach the point where they can do this for themselves as they do their pre-writing thinking.

This activity can also serve to introduce or revisit second person writing (the you-voice). This is a relatively little used form but does create the sense of immediately hooking the reader into the narrative: the narrator speaks directly to the reader, who becomes an active participant in the story/description etc.

Here are some practice sentences. Invite children to create more of their own.

1. He saw it move among the trees and crouched down, not wishing to be identified yet.
2. Karl counted out ten. Alex shrugged his shoulders, turned and left the room.
3. The TV was on, volume high, in the empty room. Suddenly the phone rang.
4. Behind Mandy's back, Tina was shaking her head. 'OK then?' Mandy wondered.
5. 'I *do* hope you'll take a little more care over this,' Miss Wilkins sighed. She reached into her handbag. They looked at each other nervously.

Association web

This is another tried and tested idea that can generate information more or less from scratch. Again you'll need to use a large sheet of paper, in the middle of which you simply write a single word – let's say 'yellow'. Then ask the children to begin linking up other words that have some association with yellow. You can strike off in various directions to create different areas of association. So we might begin by putting yellow – sun – holiday – romance – trust – deception/yellow – butter – rural – farmhouse – isolated – burglar – kidnap – past injustice/yellow – cowardice – conflict – war – courage – loyalty.

A useful feature of this technique is that children can come back to the web time and again and either concentrate on a particular cluster of associations or run their eyes over the whole thing and add an idea here and there. Creating an association web in a group will generate some unexpected insights based on other people's ideas.

sunlight flickering through leaves

trees and ferns　　　water dripping from leaves

cold damp air　　slippy rocks　　　white rapids

fast flowing

misty　　　　　　　　　　greeny-blue water

They arrived at the river　wide, hard to cross

five people　　　plane crashed

exhausted, no food　　just a few small weapons

must find shelter　danger

storm coming　　　　　　　　being chased

must cross river　by mercenaries

FIG 3.3　Association web

A variation of the idea is to write a sentence that will form the 'seed' of a story in the middle of the sheet and invite children to contribute further ideas. This can either be a whole class or group activity. A feature that this technique shares with stories themselves is that they grow 'organically', through insight and intuition as well as more conscious reasoning and decision-making. A meaningful scenario will unfold as the children's ideas accumulate. Notice how glancing at the association web now, even though it is incomplete, can spark off further ideas that may well motivate some children to go away and write – not necessarily a polished story, but perhaps as a way of further clarifying their thoughts.

Another benefit of the association web is that it is very inclusive. All children are invited to contribute something, however small a snippet, and can do so safely. Even the least confident child in the class could add 'fast flowing' without fear of ridicule or being told he is wrong. His small contribution, given that it is consistent with what has previously been written, can be valued.

Word ripples

According to the Merriam-Webster online dictionary, there are around a million words in the English language (although some linguists say this may be a large overestimate). Whatever the total, it includes thousands of scientific and technical terms that would most likely be known and used only by specialists in the field. Another aspect of assessing the 'size' of a language is that some words have a range of different meanings: 'set' apparently carries 464 while 'run', used just as a verb, has 645 (though again estimates vary). Presumably each meaning would count as a word in itself, rather than say 'run' with all its variations being regarded as a single word. A further problem is that new words are constantly being added – 'app' for instance is now commonly regarded as a word in itself – Apple launched its app store in 2008 and used it then – rather than an abbreviation or a contraction of 'application'. By the same token, there is a slow leakage of words out of the language as they fall into disuse for whatever reason. It would be interesting to see how many people in your school know the meaning of 'wittol', 'drysalter', 'charabanc' and 'alienism' for instance.

In the context of children's self-confidence, it's worth noting that *all* of us have a relatively small vocabulary when it comes to the number of words that exist in a given language. There is no shame therefore in knowing just a fraction of them (and actively using even less).

On the other hand, cultivating an interest in words and where they come from boosts children's confidence when writing. Trying out newly learned words can give children a sense of ownership as they work to develop the craft of using language eloquently. Sharing the meanings and origins of words feeds into the ethos of the 'community of writers' that we touched on earlier and helps children to develop a sense of the 'web of language' as they make creative connections between words that they might previously have thought of as separate.

Help children to become curious about words:

- Put a word like 'run' in the centre of a display board and invite children to come up with sentences that use it in a variety of different ways.

- Increase the WOW factor of the language by giving some facts and figures – that there are around a million words in English; that the average adult has a vocabulary of 20,000–35,000 words; that the average eight-year-old has a vocabulary of 10,000 words (type 'how many words in the average vocabulary' into your search engine for a range of estimates).

- Highlight the fact that we are all still learning about language by using the ripple diagram below. Again this could become a display with children adding their favourite words that they use often, newly learned or discovered words etc.

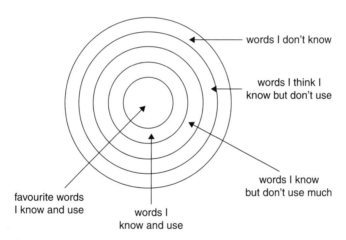

FIG 3.4 Word ripples

- Invite children who have hobbies or specialist knowledge to share some of the subject-specific words that interest them. (As a keen, though all too often armchair, amateur astronomer one of my favourite words is 'Zubenelgenubi'. This is the name of the brightest star in the constellation of Libra and is an Arabic word meaning 'Southern Claw', dating from a time before Libra was recognised as being distinct from the constellation of Scorpio the scorpion.)

- Explore the origins of words related to language and writing. 'Word' for instance goes back to Old Norse meaning to speak or say. 'Write' has its origins in Old English meaning to score, outline or draw the figure of.

Story cards

These consist of a small number of visual panels that suggest either a complete story or part of a narrative. They can be made from cut outs from comic books, pieces of clip art, images from the internet etc.

FIG 3.5   Story card (see Bloomsbury Online Resource 3C)

Children can also draw their own story cards to put towards a resource bank for future use. See **Bloomsbury Online Resource 3C** for printable story cards to download for use in your classroom.

Story cards can be used in a number of ways:

- Summarise the story (or extract) featured on the card.

- Add dialogue where appropriate.

- Think about alternative endings. Draw or write a different ending to the story.

- If this were a longer story, what would the extra panels contain?

- Use all of your senses to imagine colours, sounds, textures, smells etc. and make a note of these.

- Imagine what might be going on outside the frame of a chosen panel. Describe what you imagine.

- Is the story being told by the story card set within a particular genre? How can you tell?

Story templates

These are an extension of the story card idea, although the emphasis here is on offering children guidance on how they might plot their story and advice on some of the details it can include.

Story templates are simply and quickly drawn visual organisers within which children can note their ideas. The size of the panels means that children must think carefully about what to include and put this in note form rather than trying to write the story at the planning stage. If they are instructed to make notes in pencil – or erasable marker if the template sheets are laminated – then changes of mind present no problem and, indeed, are to be encouraged.

The relative simplicity of a story template means that children can easily draw their own. Note that story templates can be very sketchy: children don't need to be able to draw well to use the technique. See Figure 3.6 on page 50 for a quest story template. Printable versions of this and other templates are available online, see **Bloomsbury Online Resource 3D**.

Templates can be used in a number of ways:

- Use a template that has already been drawn but change the genre of the story. For example, the Story template (Figure 3.6) is a Fantasy story. What changes would you make if it was a Science Fiction tale? A murder mystery? A story set in the Wild West?

- Create a template from a story that has already been written. Or choose a film or comic that you have enjoyed as the basis for your template.

- Swap templates with a classmate. Use what you're given to plan and write the story.

- Think about how you could change a story template that you have been given. Is there something you could add to it or take away? In the Quest example, if the hero had four challenges rather than two, what would the others be and how might the hero succeed with them? If the 'friend' character needed to help the hero at two important points in the story, how might they do this?

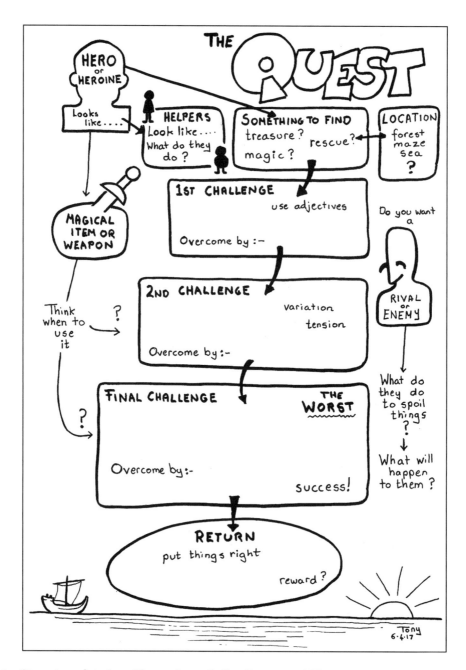

FIG 3.6 Story template (see Bloomsbury Online Resource 3D)

Clues grid

This is a grid of 36 words or phrases. It can be used in various ways.

The TV is on standby	There is two days' worth of mail in the hallway	An empty milkbottle stands on the kitchen worktop	The number of the house is 42	Ten years ago the garden shed burned down	A cup of cold coffee is on the side table in the lounge
The Phillips family lives here	The children's school is two miles away	The boxroom upstairs is always kept locked	There is an oil stain on the drive	Three pink rose bushes and a red one grow in the back garden	The DVD machine records the same programme each week
The son is twelve years old	Mrs Phillips collects stamps and old books	There are fresh footprints in the flower border	Mr Phillips had a plumbing business that went bankrupt	A telephone number has been scrawled on the wall by the phone	Flowers in the front room have died
The lock on the garden shed has been forced	A bottle of milk in the kitchen has gone sour	The bulb at the top of the stairs has failed	The bed in the main bedroom is unmade	There are a week's worth of newspapers by the bed	The spare house key is missing from the hook in the hallway
A faded red stain can be seen on the stair carpet	Mr Phillips's old school friend called round two days ago	There is money in a tin on the mantel piece in the lounge	The family owns a very valuable pedigree cat	Neighbours say the family keeps itself to itself	A guidebook to New Zealand lies on the coffee table in the front room
The family cat is undernourished	A bill from the family solicitor lies open on the hall table	Mr Phillips' star sign is Leo	There are three unanswered messages on the voicemail	It is mid-July	A locked drawer in the dresser has been forced

FIG 3.7 Clues grid

Start at the top right hand corner. Roll a die and count that number along the top row. Let's say we roll a 3 – 'An empty milkbottle stands on the kitchen worktop.' Imagine this is how the story starts. You can either simply note the clue and roll the die again, or use the sentence as the basis for an association web to 'flesh out' the beginning of the story.

Let's say the next dice roll is a 5. At the end of the first row, drop down a row and move along the second row right-to-left. A 5 gives us – 'Three pink rose bushes and a red one grow in the back garden'. Again, either simply note the clue or use it to enrich the association web that you have already started. If you are not building an association web, think about how clues one and two might be linked: what plot begins to emerge by putting them together? The activity proceeds using further dice rolls to zig-zag down the grid (like Snakes & Ladders in reverse), gathering a string of clues to suggest a plot or to develop the association web.

Print out copies of the grid on large sheets of paper (see **Bloomsbury Online Resource 3E**). Cut out the clues and, working in groups, organise some or all of them to suggest a plot. Add further clues as necessary.

Picture grid

The zig-zag technique can also be used with a picture grid such as the one shown here. See **Bloomsbury Online Resource 3F** for more picture grids.

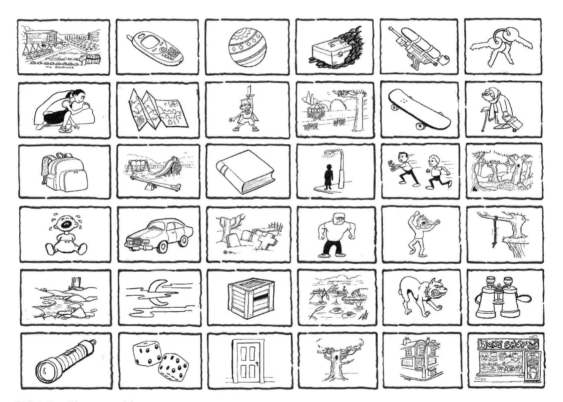

FIG 3.8   Picture grid

A more sophisticated activity is to use dice rolls to pick the coordinates of various pictures at random to begin plotting a narrative.

1. Start at the bottom left hand corner. Use dice rolls to select two images. Once you have these, link them to suggest the opening of a story or a basic story idea. Let's say we roll 2–4 'an adventure playground' and 3–5 'a boy playing knights'. The most obvious link is that a young boy is playing knights in the park.

2. Now ask an open question, such as, 'What happens next?'. Roll the die to select a third image that answers the question or gives a clue to the answer: 5–6 'a super soaker'. So the next bit of the story is where some older children come along and drench the boy with their super soaker.

3. Now ask another open question, such as, 'What does the boy do about this?'. Roll the die to select a further image that answers the question or gives a clue to the answer: 5-1 'he decides to take the quickest way home, which is along the High Street'. (But I notice that image 6-1 is a joke shop. So the boy could decide to buy some jokes or tricks to use on the children who soaked him.)

When children play this game, once they begin to firm up the plot they will tend to select images for themselves to add to the story. This is fine, though it's important that they continue to use dice rolls too, as this 'takes the mind by surprise' and allows them to make creative connections that they might not otherwise have thought about.

The game proceeds by asking further open questions followed by dice rolls that select images randomly. The activity continues until children have the basic plot of their story worked out.

Top tip

Once the story begins to grow, a useful question to ask is, 'How will it end?'. Roll the die to select an image that will answer the question or give a clue to the answer. Once a child has the early part of the story worked out and also has an idea of how it might end, he will usually find it much easier to fit further pictures (chosen himself or selected randomly) into the narrative.

For more information on this technique plus a selection of different grids see *Developing Literacy and Creative Writing Through Storymaking* (see the Bibliography for full details).

Cherry picking

This activity asks children to look at the techniques used by other writers and try to emulate them. Such techniques might be the use of vivid descriptive details, an interesting and unusual simile or metaphor, the use of exaggeration etc. Here are some from a Year 5 class:

● The writer used the metaphor 'thistly' to describe the feel of a raw wind. Children came up with barbed-wire wind, sandpaper wind, bristly wind, thorny wind. Then we experimented more widely and invented vanilla wind, candyfloss wind, kitten-fur wind, featherdown wind, carousel wind (the child had in mind the rush of the wind and the up-and-down gusty sense of it, as though riding on a carousel).

- The writer used 'port-and-lemon' to describe some women in a pub. We identified the technique as using something a particular kind of person has or does as a descriptive phrase. Children came up with spritzer girls, pint-and-a-pie men, white wine women, pipe and slippers men, a labradoodle kind of family. We used this as an opportunity to discuss the pros and cons of stereotyping. The children understood that stereotypes are generalisations but decided that sometimes they could be used because most people know what they mean.

- The writer used exaggeration and a couple of descriptive details to create a thumbnail sketch of a character. For instance, 'Brian was a big, square-looking kid with a big square head and not much of a neck. He had legs like tree trunks'. The children from one group created Mr Dee who was 'plump and wore colourful jackets. He looked like a beach ball'. Finally 'Mrs Pettifer who was 'very thin and had a mass of frizzy hair. She looked like a stick of candyfloss'.

Chapter 4
Practice pieces

Asking children to work through various exercises has long been a standard strategy in helping them to understand some of the technical aspects of the language. However, it is only one way among many of helping young writers to learn. Consider supplementing more typical exercise work with less conventional activities to sharpen their skills.

Spot the error

Ask the children if they can see what kind of mistake is being made in the sentences below. Invite them to create further examples for themselves.

1. I was sick and fed up of being frightened and scared, so decided to do something about it.

Tautology – saying the same thing twice; sick, fed up, frightened, scared (although some children might argue they refer to different emotions, in which case the point is worth discussing).

2. I decided that I liked Edgar. He was around 50 I'd guess, so several years older than Mum, and his face was what you'd call cosy rather than good looking. It was a friendly face, and his eyes were gentle and caring. I hoped they stayed together.

Misplaced pronoun – grammatically 'they' refers to Edgar's eyes, whereas the intention was for 'they' to refer to Edgar and Mum.

3. The stream trickled up over the hill and tumbled down into the valley below.

Error of logic – the stream couldn't trickle 'up over the hill'.

4. Gluteus Maximus the centurion looked at his watch to check how long his cohort of soldiers had been on the march.

Anachronism – an error regarding time. Watches did not exist in Roman times.

5. The glasses were found by the murdered man's body.

Ambiguity – the sentence could mean either that the glasses were found beside the murdered man's body, or that the murdered man's body found the glasses.

6. I need someone reliable, trustworthy and sensible, but you'll do.
I need someone reliable, trustworthy and sensible, so you'll do.

Clarity of meaning – substituting 'but' with 'so' completely alters the meaning of the sentence. 'But' suggests that the person is not reliable, trustworthy etc. while 'so' indicates that he is.

7. Mr Lenditt: So last time we met you said that your bank balance was healthy. Is that right?
Mr C. Card: Yes.

Ambiguity: Is it right that he said that, or is it right that his bank balance is healthy?

8. In exactly thirty seconds it will be approximately 1.15.
After this announcement we will continue with our uninterrupted programme of music.

Contradictions: Exactly and approximately contradict one another. The uninterrupted programme was interrupted.

9. Lost, an octagonal lady's gold bracelet. £25 reward.

Unintended meaning: Grammatically, 'octagonal' refers to the lady not the bracelet, as intended.

Logically speaking

An important aspect of the writer's craft is to make the story work in terms of its internal consistency and logic. The examples above touch on this at a sentence level in terms of achieving clarity of meaning. Here are some tougher puzzlers that call for a dose of logical thinking.

1) "All Martians are always liars," said the Martian.

Is the Martian speaking the truth? This is a version of the so-called 'liar paradox'. If the statement is true that all Martians are always liars then the Martian who spoke is also a liar. But if he is a liar (as all Martians always are) then the statement can't be true. But if the statement is a lie than it supports the assertion that all Martians are liars.

2) The police discover John Doe dead in his flat. Beside him are a gun which has recently been fired and a digital voice recorder. Inspector Broom of the Yard sees that the gun has been fired just once. Then he presses the Play button of the recorder. The recorder replays a suicide message then the sound of the gun being fired. Inspector Broom knows at once that this is a murder case. How?

Inspector Broom had to press the play button to start the recorder. If John Doe had shot himself he would not have been alive to press stop; someone else – presumably the murderer – did this.

3) Albert Hall loved the colour yellow. All the walls of his new bungalow were painted a lovely daffodil yellow. The carpets and curtains and all the soft furnishings were in different shades of yellow. What colour was his stair carpet?

Albert Hall lived in a bungalow, so there was no stair carpet.

4) You enter a deserted house late at night. Inside are an oil lamp, a gas fire and a wood burning stove. You have only one match. Which should you light first?

The match. (That is so sneaky!)

5) In 1492 Christopher Columbus discovered America.

What is wrong with this sentence? In 1492 the continent had not been named America. To be correct it should read 'In 1492 Christopher Columbus discovered the continent that would later be named America.' (Also, did he 'discover' America, seeing as there were already people living there? Another interesting point to discuss with your class.)

6) Following a tip-off, a team of FBI agents burst into a house to arrest a suspected murderer. All they know is that his name is Ben. When the agents arrive they find two plumbers, a lorry driver and a bank manager playing poker. They immediately arrest the lorry driver. How did they know this was Ben?

The other poker players were women.

7) A Roman coin dated 254 B.C. is being sold on the Internet for a bargain price. The seller claims it is genuine. Is he right?

No, because B.C. (Before Christ) could not appear on the coin before Christ lived.

8) Mr Smith built a house where all the windows faced South. How was this possible?

He built it at the North Pole.

9) Two Scrabble champions played five games of Scrabble. They each won and lost the same number of games and there were no draws. How can this be?

They were not playing against one another but against different opponents.
    And a nice easy one to finish…

10) Which sentence is correct – 'The yolk of an egg is white' or 'The yolk of an egg are white'?

Neither because the yolk of an egg is yellow.
    Confession: I couldn't figure out most of these when I first came across them!

Public domain pieces

A huge amount of literature exists in the public domain and is free of copyright (for example from www.gutenberg.org or www.librivox.org, where you can also hear audio versions of many of the texts). Thus you can download and reproduce extracts, short stories etc. for children to study. Encourage them to explore the text by using the 'cloud of questions and observations' techniques explained below. These help to establish the habit of engaging with writing (rather than being passive recipients of facts about it) and serve as a bridge to the more formal analysis of text and literary criticism. Children also quickly learn that asking questions is not a sign of ignorance but rather an intelligent behaviour motivated by the desire to learn more.

A cloud of observations

Begin by showing the class an ordinary everyday object. Invite children to notice anything about it and when they have done so, to say what they have noticed. Assure them that no observation will be considered trivial. Encourage children to use all of their senses in this activity. So if you showed them a coffee mug, invite children to hold it, tap it with a fingernail, a pencil, a spoon etc. Make a point of giving credit when small or subtle details have been observed.

Note: Although this activity is simple, it is 'safe'. If by chance a child misidentifies a detail, give them the opportunity to check. Often they will correct themselves (rather than you doing it). Follow this up with 'Well done, you had the common sense to look again and the confidence to change your mind'.

Asking children to pay attention in this way and to notice details allows them to practise a skill that is useful in all sorts of other ways, not least in their writing. The inclusion of small but vivid details immediately enriches a piece of work, while spotting instances of incorrect or absent punctuation obviously improves the technical aspects of their writing.

A cloud of questions

Begin by showing the class an ordinary everyday object. Invite them to ask any questions they like about it. There is no expectation that they (or you) will know any of the answers. This tactic alone helps children to feel less vulnerable about getting anything wrong. Having said that, if you sense that they feel inhibited in case they ask a 'silly' question, use quotes to shift that unhelpful attitude:

> 'The "silly question" is the first intimation of some totally new development', Alfred North Whitehead, mathematician and philosopher.

> 'There are no foolish questions and no one becomes a fool until he has stopped asking questions', Charles Proteus Steinmetz, mathematician and electrical engineer.

> 'Students are not here to worship what is known, but to question it', Jacob Bronowski, biologist and historian of science.

> 'Wonder is the seed of knowledge,' Francis Bacon, philosopher, statesman, scientist and author.

The cloud of questions activity helps to shift children's behaviour away from being just passive recipients of facts. It also familiarises them further with the power of open questions, helping them to realise that even a relatively simple where-when-what-who-why-how question can open up rich avenues of further exploration.

On a personal note, it surprised me at first how much I didn't know about so many everyday objects. Where does the word 'mug' come from? Why is coffee so called? When were drinking vessels first invented? Why are coffee mugs made from pottery? Where does the word 'clay' come from? How many coffee mugs are there in the world? Who invented instant coffee? And so on – and on! Being in such a position of 'unknowing' was a salutary experience for me, but it did put me in mind of a piece of advice a teacher friend once gave me – a good teacher is never afraid to say in response to a question, 'I don't know, but how could we find out?'.

Take this activity further by asking the children to categorise the questions that have been asked. Take some time to explore what the most useful categories might be, again explaining that there are no single right or definitive answers. In a school where I ran this activity, children suggested classifications such as:

1. Really interesting questions.
2. Questions that are easy to find the answers to.
3. Questions that are hard to find the answers to.
4. Questions that are impossible to answer.
5. Questions that have a right answer but you could never find it out.
6. Questions that can have more than one answer.
7. Questions that someone in the class already knew the answer to.
8. Questions that lead to other questions.

Question tree

That last category (8. Questions that lead to further questions) is especially useful because it gives children a sense of direction in their active questioning around a topic and creates the opportunity for some extended research if you or they want to chase up some answers. The question 'Who invented instant coffee' was an off-branch of the earlier question about why coffee is so called. The class I worked with created a question tree as a visual display to show not just the questions they asked but how such questions were related. We put the word 'coffee' at the base of the trunk and gave each of the big open question words its own colour-coded main branch. Smaller branches came off these representing sub-categories of questions. We numbered these (as above). So 'who invented instant coffee' was a twig coming off the blue main branch (we decided 'blue for who') and had the numbers 1 and 7 appended to it. Answers, where these could be found, were written on paper leaves. Some questions whose answers could not be found were ripe for speculation and inference. Children's ideas in these instances were noted on pieces of paper in the shape of fruit (being 'ripe' for speculation).

The question tree activity brings other educational benefits besides gathering facts. Children learn to question the reliability of their sources of information, to double check facts, to tease out fact from opinion or conjecture and to become more comfortable with ambiguity, uncertainty and simply not knowing answers that cannot be uncovered. The activity also encourages *active questioning* – following a question trail that can lead into further realms of knowledge – and helps children to reflect on different strategies for finding information.

Having run the cloud of observations/questions activity several times, ask children to apply the same techniques to chunks of text. These can be placed on one side of the page with the children's responses on the other. The activity can also be applied to poetry and pieces of non-fiction, and can be extended by asking children to find answers to their questions that can be added to the text in the form of foot- or margin-notes.

Excerpt from A Christmas Carol	Questions and observations on the text
When Scrooge awoke, it was so dark, that looking out of bed, he could scarcely distinguish the transpateat window from the opaque walls of his chamber. He was endeavouring to pierce the darkness with his ferret eyes, when the chimes of a oeighhouring church struck the four quarters. So he listened for the hour. To his great astonishment the heavy bell went on from six to seven and from seven to eight, and regularly up to twelve; then stopped Twelve! It was past two when he went to bed. The clock was wrong. An icicle must have got into the works. Twelve! He touched the spring of his repeater, to correct this most preposterous clock. Its rapid little pulse beat twelve, and stopped. "Why, it isn't possible," said Scrooge "that I can have slept through a whole day and far into another night. It isn't possible that anything has happened to the sun, and this is twelve at noon!" The idea being an alarming one, he scrambled out of bed, and groped his way to the window. He was obliged to rub the frost off with the sleeve of his dressing-gown before he could see anything and could see very little then. All he could make out was, that it was still very foggy and extremely cold, and that there was no noise of people running to and fro, and making a great stir, as there unquestionably would have been if night had beaten off bright day, and taken possession of the world. This was a great relief because "Three days after sight of this First of Exchange pay to Mr. Ebenezer Scrooge or his order," and so forth, would have become a mere United States security if there were no days to count by. crooge went to bed again, and thought, and thought, and thought it over and over and over, and could make nothing of it. The more he thought, the more perplexed he was; and, the more he endeavoured not to think, the more he thought. Marley's Ghost bothered him exceedingly. Every time he resolved within himself, after mature inquiry, that it was all a dream, his mind flew back again, like a strong spring released, to it first position, and presented the same problem to be worked all through, "Was it a dream or not?"	Who is Scrooge? What doe the name mean – is it like calling a mean person 'a sorooge' What does 'opaque' mean? 'struck the four quarters' makes it sound old fashioned Is this meant to be funny? What is a 'repeater'? (Maybe same kind of clock?) Must be winter time. Why doesn't he have heating in his room? (Maybe can't afford it?) Don't understand this sentence. Is 'perplexed' the same as 'puzzled'? Simile.

FIG 4.1 Public domain pieces, from Charle Dickens' *A Christmas Carol*

Minisagas

A minisaga is a short story of exactly 50 words (though you may allow extra for the title). Writing minisagas can be good fun, while the fact that they seemingly don't involve much work often tempts more reluctant writers to have a go. The real challenge of a minisaga is the careful choice of words. At their first attempt many children will over-write, so the main task is to edit down to the word count you've specified. Practising minisagas develops the skill of concise writing, highlights the notion of 'words that do plenty of work' and sharpens children's editing skills.

Top tip
A variation of the activity is to give children minisagas prepared beforehand that are intentionally over the word count. The emphasis then is on editing rather than creating the plot.

Here are a few 50-word stories:

1. A sly thief ignored the misspelling on the treasure map. He followed it to the gnarled oak. Beneath the roots were gold and jewels. He dug, uncovering a fortune. Suddenly, a buzz, a sting. Then a deep droning and an attacking swarm. He died realising his mistake – Here, bee dragons.

2. Milton Spilk stole a fortune, left his wife and kids and ran off with a younger woman. They lived the high life until the money was gone then she vanished like morning mist. A sad story? No, he surely deserved it. In any case we shouldn't cry over Milt Spilk.

3. The cricket match at Upper Magna was a complete disaster. The wicket keeper discovered that one of the stumps had been mislaid. Despite searching everywhere, no joy. "It's not my fault!" he complained. But everyone just kept nagging. "I can't help it if there is no piece for the wicket."

4. Earth was in crisis. What remained of humanity went to the freezing rooms; slept while the radiation faded. Thousands of years passed by. Connor woke first, groggy, confused. Nearby shadows moved. Something leaped towards him holding a knife. A rat the size of a man. There were thousands! Nature's revenge.

This last example is over-written in its first version. Ask the children how they would alter it to fit it into the 50-word format. My attempt to edit it follows below. See **Bloomsbury Online Resource 4A** for more over-length minisagas for on-screen editing activities.

5. This was much worse than the scariest dare that Nige had ever tried. Please let the car break down! Please let Auntie Myra be out shopping! Please let Mum change her mind! But no, the visit was happening. Drive across town, walk up the garden path, knock on the front door. Agh, she's there! "Ooo, come here my lovely little nephew." And she gave Nige a big wet sloppy kiss on the mouth. How embarrassing! (75 words)

Much worse than the scariest dare Nige had ever tried. Let the car break down! Let Mum change her mind! But no, it's happening – across town, up the path, knock on front door. Auntie's there. "Ooo my lovely little nephew. Come here!" Big wet kiss on mouth. How embarrassing!

Refining editing skills

Traditionally children have produced pieces of work that the teacher has marked; pointing out technical errors, correcting mistakes as necessary and commenting on areas of improvement and positive aspects of the writing. This is a necessary and useful process but one that can become more powerful and versatile when we ask the children themselves to edit examples of their own and others' work. Giving them increasingly sophisticated 'editing challenges' sharpens up their critical thinking, creates the opportunity to revisit a range of points covered in the English curriculum and, ultimately, allows children to enjoy a greater sense of ownership over what they produce. Giving the class complete stories to edit also creates a more meaningful context for them to practise their editing skills.

Begin by using pieces that have not been written by the children themselves: this helps them to feel that they are not being personally criticised. As they grow in confidence, keeping in mind their writer's rights and responsibilities (page 16–17), encourage children to comment on their own and their classmates' work. If the ethos of the classroom explored in Chapter 1 has been established, children are much more likely to feel supported and motivated to reflect on their writing at all stages of its production – thinking time, writing time as well as looking back time.

Flag up the errors

Show children a short story or piece of non-fiction containing some deliberate errors. These might relate to recent lessons on spelling, punctuation, grammar, narrative structure etc. Mark these in the text and ask children to explain what's amiss. Subsequently, show the class another piece of writing with the same errors, but unmarked. If run as a whole-class activity, less confident children will feel safer in their anonymity than if every child is asked to point out mistakes individually. Even so, some children might initially feel criticised if they misidentify an error, though my experience has been that when the learning environment is supportive and positive these feelings tend to disappear.

The following short stories are available as editable stories online; see **Bloomsbury Online Resource 4B**.

The Man Who Walked Backwards

One day Tony and Tanzie were strolling along in the countryside when they came upon a most unusual sight. In the distance was a man who appeared to be walking backwards. He had an open rucksack across his shoulders and an intense look of concentration on his face. He was stooping low and seemed to be studying the ground very carefully (1)

   "What is he doing?" Tony wanted to know.

   Tanzie, practical as ever, said, "Well lets' (2) go and ask him shall we?"

▶

As the children drew closer they sore (3) that the man was picking up stones from the path and tossing them into his rucksack. It looked to be quite full of rocks and pebbles of various sizes and must surely be quite a burden to bare. (4)

"But why –" Tony began, when Tanzie interrupted him with a shout.

"Look out!" she whispered cautiously. (5)

The backwards walking man had been so busy in his task that he'd failed to see a deep pothole behind him. Now, as he added another stone to his collection and took a further step backwards, his foot went into the hole and he toppled in and fell with a crash. Stones spilled out of his rucksack and the air gushed from his lungs with a great whoosh. The children rushed up to help him.

"Here sir, (6) said Ian (7), "let me give you a hand." With Tony's assistance the man struggled to his feet while Tanzie retrieved the rucksack, which had fallen from his shoulders, and laid it at his feet.

"Thank you indeed," said the man.

"You're very welcome," Tanzie replied. "Although I suppose it must happen quite often if you don't look where you are going." She did not mean to be rude and the man seemed not to be offended.

"Well," he explained, "I can see where I've been. And that's very important."

"But why do you pick up the stones, (8)" Tony blurted out. The man looked serious.

"It's my path and I'm responsible for it. I can't have a stony path, can I now?"

"Paths always have stones on them," Tanzie said with a child's simple logic. "And of course they can trip you up and get in your shoes and make walking uncomfortable. But that's just how stones are and there's no getting away from it!"

This gave the man pause for thought. "Hm, there's something in that," he pondered.

"And of course," Tony added, adding (9) to what Tanzie had said, "there will always be more stones along the way than you could possibly deal with. No one could ever collect them all and make the path perfectly smooth and safe."

"Hmmmm," the man said again, his mind full of big thoughts now.

"So wouldn't it make better sense just to lay down your rucksack and take that weight of (10) your shoulders?"

This idea was like a brilliant light to the man. His face glowed with happiness and he beamed a huge smile at the children. "Thank you, thank you so much for helping me to see that. You're right! I'll simply leave that old rucksack where it is!"

So he did just that and, with a wave to Tony and Tanzie, the man continued walking backwards on his way.

Errors:

1. No full stop.
2. Should be 'let's'.
3. Should be 'saw'.
4. Should be 'bear'.
5. The text says Tanzie shouted, but then her words are tagged 'she whispered cautiously'. This is a contradiction.

6. Missing speech marks.

7. 'Ian' should be 'Tony'.

8. Missing question mark.

9. 'Tony added, adding' is clumsy repetition. Suggest 'replied, adding…'

10. Should be 'off'.

Here is a different story with the same errors, but not marked.

The Scariest Dare

Nigel Lloyd was the leader of our group of friends. We called ourselves the Double Darers The idea was that we would dare each other to do things, but whoever made up the dare would be double dared back by the rest of us. Then everyone had to do the dare. Sometimes Nigel would announce a Super Dare. This was something that usually went on all week. It would start with a group huddle in the playground when we had all arrived at school on the Monday morning.

We knew there would be a Super Dare this week because of the grin on Nigel's face. "Come on then," I said, "lets' hear it."

We huddled-up and Nige told us about the dare. Kev burst into nervous laughter and Anthony looked as though he was going to be sick. We all broke away from the huddle and backed off going, 'Nooo – nooo…' Even Brian who was big and square-looking with a big square head and not much of a neck who stood like a wall and was our loyal bodyguard went, 'Nooo – nooo…'

"I never sore any of you looking so terrified before." Nigel laughed.

"I can't bare even to think about it!" I yelled quietly.

Man up guys, Nige said.

The reason for our fear was because the Super Dare involved the scariest kid in the school, who was this girl called Angie Major. Now if you happen to know anyone called Angie, <u>this</u> Angie will be totally different. Angie Major was huge – I mean, big and powerful with muscles. She was super strong and incredibly fierce. Angie played hockey for the girls' A team. She'd wanted to play rugby on the boys' team but all of the boys were scared of her so she had to settle for hockey.

Like I said, Angie was big and strong and ferocious! At break time she would stand with her friends out on the playing field doing the girlie-gossip thing with her arms folded and her face thrust forward like some terrifying nightclub bouncer.

Anyway, to get to the point. Angie had masses of fiery red hair like Boudicca (we'd just finished a project on Boudicca in History). She used to do her hair up in long plaits tied off with little green ribbons at the end. Nigel's Super Dare was that each morning break, one of us would have to sneak up on Angie, tug those pigtails and try to get away.

So you can see why we all went, 'Nooo – nooo!'

Ian was expecting this of course. His face broke into one of his famous big grins and he said, "You know what I'm going to say don't you. <u>I'm daring you</u>."

It was Anthony who opened his mouth and put his foot in it because without even thinking or reasoning it out he said, "Yeah, well we're double daring you!" And then he realised what he'd said and started to cry.

Nige took out his dice (he always kept one handy in his pocket: he used to say, 'I call it a dice because I never say die') and we each rolled it to see what order we'd do the dare.

I rolled a one.

"Can't we call the whole thing of?" I said, without hope.

So that morning break there's Angie and her friends doing to girlie-gossip thing out on the playing fields. There're the other Double Darers round the corner by our classroom going, 'Tee-hee-tee-hee, he's got to go first.' There's me strolling along minding my own business, gazing at the clouds, whistling a tuneless melody… But I ask you, have you ever <u>tried</u> to look innocent? It doesn't work. Although I was getting pretty close and thought I might just get away with it. But I must have looked a bit suspicious and I guess one of Angie's friends whispered in her ear –

Because as I reached up to pull her pigtails Angie whipped her head round really fast and lashed me across the face with those plaits. In shock I fell backwards on to the grass. Then Angie gave a great bellowing roar and belly-flopped right down on top of me.

OOF!

And before I could wriggle free she gave me a big wet kiss on the mouth – suh-MAK!

It wouldn't have been so bad but she'd just finished eating a packet of salt and vinegar crisps. I tasted them all day.

It was all so embarrassing that afterwards none of the other Double Darers would dare to do it, so for the rest of the week they were all Yellow Belly Chickens and I wasn't!

But what a price to pay…

*

Errors:

1. No full stop.
2. Should be 'let's'.
3. Should be 'saw'.
4. Should be 'bear'.
5. The text says 'yelled quietly'. This is a contradiction.
6. Missing speech marks.
7. 'Ian' should be 'Nigel'.
8. Missing question mark.
9. Should be 'off'.

Before and after

Another technique is to use before-and-after pieces of text. Ask the children to notice what changes the author has made and to suggest why he or she might have made them. Also invite children to say if they would have made any other/different alterations to the text.

This example is the blurb from a short story collection called 'Tales of Arthur King'.

Before –
Twelve-year-old Arthur King lives in a world of his own, of daydreams and stories. It is a world filled with dragons and wizards, ghosts and monsters, magic and doorways through time.

Arthur and his best friend Melvin Phipps love to visit lonely and out-of-the-way places where they live in the Rhondda Valley of South Wales – windblown hilltops, woodlands and rocky outcrops where their imaginations can fly.

The boys' adventures take them to a sunny afternoon frozen forever in time. They meet a boy who, because no one notices him, is in danger of fading out of existence. They hear of a rag-and-bone man who returns from the dead to stop his property being stolen. They find an old house in the woods that is a doorway to many wonderful worlds…

Perhaps these are the last great daydreams of childhood, though sometimes Arthur and Melvin wonder where reality ends and fantasy begins.

After –
Twelve-year-old Arthur King lives in a world of his own, a world of daydreams and stories filled with dragons and wizards, ghosts and monsters, magic and doorways through time.

Arthur and his best friend Melvin Phipps love to visit out-of-the-way places where they live in the Rhondda Valley of South Wales – windblown hilltops, lonely woodlands and rocky outcrops where their imaginations can fly.

The boys' adventures take them to a sunny afternoon frozen forever in time. They meet a boy who, because no one notices him, is in danger of fading out of existence. They hear of a rag-and-bone man who returns from the dead to stop his property being stolen. They find an old house in the woods that hides a doorway to many wonderful worlds…

Perhaps these are only the last great daydreams of childhood, though don't we all wonder sometimes where fantasy ends and reality begins?

Task:

- What changes have been made?
- Why do you think the author made those changes?
- What changes would you make any why?

Here are some comments from Year 6 pupils.

'The author has rearranged the words to make it easier to read and to make the blurb more interesting.' – Chloe.

'The second sentence in the final draft misses out the word lonely, but the author has used it later. Personally I would remove the phrase lonely and replace it with mysterious as this further builds suspense and excitement.' – Jayden.

'The author talks about a sunny afternoon frozen in time but I think sunny-frozen is a contrast and would replace it with – a sunny afternoon locked in time.' – Lucy.

'The phrase "hides a doorway to many wonderful worlds" flows much better than what the author wrote in the first draft.' – Alex.

'There is more detail in the second version. We think the author did this to give readers a better view. We wouldn't make any changes to the final draft because it is fine as it is.' – Dylan and Katie.

'Different adjectives have been put in the second version to improve the sentences. I wouldn't change anything about the second draft.' – Paige.

'I think the author has done these two versions to give us a task to do!' – Mark.

Track changes

If children write on a computer, suggest that they use the 'track changes' function in their word processing program. This reinforces the learning value of changes-of-mind. A variation of the activity is to supply children with a piece of text and ask them to make any alterations that they think would improve the writing, later commenting on the tracked changes.

Here are the alterations that Lucas suggested.

Twelve-year-old Arthur King lives in a world of his own, a world full of daydreams and stories filled with dragons, and wizards, ghosts, and monsters, magic and doorways through time.

Arthur and his best friend Melvin Phipps love to visit deserted out-of-the-way places where they live in the Rhondda Valley of South Wales — windblown hilltops, lonely woodlands and rocky outcrops where their imaginations can fly.

The boys' adventures take them to a sunny afternoon frozen forever in time. They meet a boy who, because no one notices him, is in danger of fading out of existence. They hear of a rag-and-bone man who returns from the dead to stop his property being stolen. They find an old house in the woods that hides a doorway to many wonderful worlds...

Perhaps these are only the last great daydreams of childhood, al though don't we all wonder sometimes where fantasy ends and reality begins?

FIG 4.2   Lucas's edits

Chapter 5
A love of language

Cultivating a love of language further motivates children to want to know how language works. As children engage with words, coming more to appreciate their power as well as their aesthetic qualities, they are more inclined to learn about the technical aspects of language: when the context and interest are there, the mechanics of language will make more sense.

Here is a selection of techniques and activities to help facilitate that.

Sounds interesting

The story card technique on page 48 asks children to imagine sounds associated with a picture. As they do this, many children actually *make* the sound they have in mind rather than just describing it. So instead of saying 'It was a long, loud screeching sound', a child might say 'SCREEEeeeeeeeee!' – often with an accompanying mime. When this happens, ask the child in question if they would try and write the sound down in that way if they were writing a story, and if so what letters would they use? (If the child says no they wouldn't, reply with 'But if you did, what letters would you use?')

Other children can be asked for their suggestions too as the child makes an effort of imagination to recreate the sound in written form. Spellings will vary but that's not important here: your agenda is to encourage children to play with sounds and match them with letter sequences; to explore sound creatively as you help them to appreciate the aural qualities of language. It is also a way of heightening children's 'phonemic awareness', albeit informally but in an enjoyable way.

Note: In her book *Why Children Can't Read – and what we can do about it,* Professor Diane McGuinness recommends the systematic teaching of phonemes in a given order as a precursor to developing reading skills, i.e. learning the range of phonemes before mapping them on to letter patterns. A technique she uses in conjunction with this is to ask children, as they make these sounds, to notice what they are doing physically. How are they shaping their lips? What is the tongue doing? Is the mouth open (by how much?) or closed? How is the air passing up through the throat? What does the throat feel like as different sounds are being made?

Heightening awareness in this way helps children to become more sensitive to the tonal qualities of the voice and is a useful early step in developing their storytelling/communication skills.

Take it further

Comics are a great resource for collecting examples of onomatopoeia, as in the famous Pow! Biff! Wham! of super hero comics.

- Ask children to bring in examples of onomatopoeic sounds and what they refer to.
- Show the class a list of 'sound effects' taken from comics and invite children to guess what is making them. Here are some examples:

DAKA-DAKA-DAKA-DAKA – the rhythm of a water pump.

KRUNK! – a metal sheet crumpling as it's hit by a heavy object.

BUDABUDABUDABUDA – a helicopter flying low overhead.

BuDOOMMmm!!! – a muffled explosion nearby and an example of where it's acceptable to use more than one exclamation mark!

Here are a few more for you to ponder over:

Rch-rch-rch-rch

Slup!

Snp-snp-snp

Thp-thp-thp-thp

- Ask children to think about why the 'comic book spelling' of an onomatopoeic word sometimes differs from its conventional spelling, as in 'krak' and 'crack'.

- The sound effects words in comics are often drawn so that their shape complements the sound being suggested. Ask children to describe the design of such words and, perhaps using some of the examples above, to 'draw them as they sound'. Add colour – what colours would children choose for their chosen words and why?

FIG 5.1   Sound effects 1, see Bloomsbury Online Resource 5A

Explore subtle distinctions between the sounds suggested by similar onomatopoeic words. For instance 'splash' is a common example but how does it differ from 'splish', 'splesh', 'splosh', 'sploosh' and 'spuh*lash*'? In other words, what is different about the liquid in each case and/or what is being dropped into it?

Top tip

Running this activity creates the opportunity for children to learn about so-called 'submodalities' or constituent features of sound. These include direction, volume, speed, pitch, tone, pauses, length and cadence (rhythmic flow of sound).

Exploring submodalities also creates the opportunity to play with adjectives such as brittle, cutting, dry, dull, faint, gentle, harsh, heavy, high, liquid, low, penetrating, raspy, rough, sharp, smooth, soft, strong, sweet.

Make a display of such descriptors so that they are visually available to children as they talk about sounds.

Notice how some describing words for sound are also applied to other senses. 'Brittle' for instance is also a tactile word, while 'sweet' refers to taste as well. This is an idea we came across in multisensory thinking on page 31.

Show the class a visual like the one in Figure 5.2 (see **Bloomsbury Online Resource 5B**). Ask them to choose a few of the words and describe how they visualise the sounds and, looking at the images – if these were sounds, what do you hear? Another way of using the visual is to say, 'This is a busy building site. Write a description of how you imagine it.' A similar activity is to play some instrumental music and say, 'If this music were a person, what would they be like? Describe that person's appearance and personality.'

Euphony

Euphony comes from the Greek meaning 'sweet-voiced' and refers to a word or combination of words that have a soothing or otherwise pleasurable effect on the ear. Its opposite is cacophony meaning 'confused noise'. While we find the notion of euphony/cacophony in music, they are also literary devices emphasising the aural qualities of words and linked with (but not exactly the same as) alliteration, assonance and onomatopoeia.

Making children more aware of words that soothe and flow and those that grate and clash gives them another way of appreciating and commenting on an aspect of stories or poems that they hear and/or read aloud for themselves and which can also be used analytically. The flow, rhythm and melody (sweet music) of language are recognised at an emotional level whether or not a child is familiar with the technical aspects of its construction.

> *'But, soft! what light through yonder window breaks?*
> *It is the east, and Juliet is the sun.*
> *Arise, fair sun, and kill the envious moon,*
> *Who is already sick and pale with grief,*
> *That thou her maid art far more fair than she.'*
> *(Romeo and Juliet, Act 2 scene 2)*

FIG 5.2   Sound effects 2, see Bloomsbury Online Resource 5B

Simply by listening carefully to these lines, many children will be able to pick up their lambent quality – and some may even spot the five-beat rhythm – without needing (yet) to be taught about iambic pentameter. Similarly:

> 'The moon shines bright. In such a night as this,
>
> When the sweet wind did gently kiss the trees…'
>
> (The Merchant of Venice, Act 5 Scene 1)

The use of soft sounding letters like m, n, w and s create a 'soundscape' that enhances the image evoked by the words.

Try altering the lines a little to see firstly if children notice any difference in the 'sound quality' of the new version, and if they are able to give reasons for their judgement. (Sacrilege perhaps to some fans of Shakespeare, but done in the noble cause of children's education!)

For example:

> 'The full moon shines brightly. In a night such as this,
>
> When the sweet wind gently kisses the trees…'

Although – to my ear – this version doesn't sound bad, the subtle soothing rhythm of the original has been lost. Metaphorically, it's the difference between gentle ripples on water and a choppy surface.

Euphonic language uses long vowels (that are more harmonious than consonants); melodious consonants like l, m, n, r and soft consonants such as soft f and v, w, s, y plus blends like th and wh.

Asking children to speak letters out loud helps to develop their phonemic awareness but more broadly 'trains the ear' which in turn deepens and enriches their understanding of language.

Explain the notion of euphony and cacophony to the class. (You may want to say that some words *sound* pleasant and others sound less pleasant.) Now show them pairs of words and ask them which word in each pair they like hearing more. It's not important if children don't know the meanings of words; in fact it helps if they don't because they can then concentrate on the aural quality of the words themselves rather than being distracted by mental imagery and associations. Here are some examples:

- beguile/hirsute
- rancid/lassitude
- obstreperous/scintilla
- penumbra/coarse
- radiant/grimace

Children might need to hear or say each pair several times before they feel they can decide.

Increase the challenge a little by asking which phrase in each pair sounds better and why. Use the examples below and/or come up with your own.

- cellar door/shed door
- grey pavement/grey wall
- brown stairs/brown bricks
- jagged stone/round moon
- rippling liquid/clattering shoes

In giving reasons for their preferences, some children might simply say one phrase 'just sounds better'. Encourage them to offer more detail by telling them about hard-soft, long-short sounds and the relative physical ease of speaking out each phrase. For instance, in the first example 'cellar door' is easier to say than 'shed door' where, if it is said properly, with the words separated (rather than 'sheddoor') we need to poke the tongue twice against the back of the teeth/front of the upper palate to pronounce the two ds. This is slightly more of an effort than saying cellar door, where the sounds seem to spill out of the mouth all by themselves. (Incidentally it is claimed that the sound of 'cellar door' (not the image it evokes) is the most euphonious combination of sounds that exists in English.)

Extend the activity further by showing full sentences and asking children to decide which they'd use in a story and why:

I'm having toast and treacle for my tea.
I'm having toast and jam for my tea.

There's only one egg left upon my plate.
There's only one tomato left on my plate.
There's only one tomato on my plate.

The wind blew through the empty quiet street.
The wind rushed through the deserted quiet street.
The wind moved like a ghost among the trees.
It was a very windy night and there was no one out and about on the street.

Two important points arise from this simple activity:

- A sense of what works

The creative aspect of writing does not end when the thinking/planning time is over. Sometimes a writer is 'in the zone' and the creative flow means that words tumble out on to the page or screen in what seems to be a polished, finished form. The sentences 'work' insofar as they have an elegance in terms of their structure and sound (as well perhaps as a freshness of perspective that conveys new images to the reader's mind). This is a very satisfying experience, one of the deep pleasures of writing. At other times, as no doubt all authors will admit, there is that mental feeling of constipation when writing is a struggle and progress is difficult and slow (or slow and difficult – which sounds better to you?).

When the creative flow appears however it is uplifting; it boosts the confidence of the writer that they 'can do it after all'. Creative flow comes with experience but I believe is never entirely under conscious control. But saying that, a willingness to engage with language, to play with word patterns and sounds hones the sensibilities and helps to develop the sense of what works at this level of sentences and paragraphs. A sense of what works at the deeper level of narrative structure requires different skills!

- Show don't tell

This is standard advice. The idea behind 'show' is to put the reader through the same experience that the character is having (and therefore that the writer had when he first imagined the scene).

So going back to the sentences:

a) The wind blew through the empty quiet street.

b) The wind rushed through the deserted quiet street.

c) The wind moved like a ghost among the trees.

d) It was a very windy night and there was no one out and about on the street.

For me, sentence d) is the weakest as it has no rhythmical quality and the reader is *told* that it was a 'very' windy night. In that regard, sentence b) is stronger because the force of the wind is suggested by 'rushed'. However, 'deserted' interrupts the rhythm established at the start. In sentence a) the rhythm is intact but 'blew' does not have the force of 'rushed'. Sentence c) is a cliché but creates a vivid visual image in the mind. If a child were writing a scary story, the simile would be especially apt.

Asking children which sentence they would choose is something of a trick question. There's no reason why children can't cherry pick from two or more sentences what they think works best, so they might end up with 'The wind rushed through the empty quiet street, moving like a ghost among the trees'. In my view, this is the strongest combination, the one from the sentences offered that most powerfully puts the reader on that street. Note too that the sentence would work equally well within a poem or a piece of narrative prose.

Round words and spiky words

Show the children this picture (see **Bloomsbury Online Resource 5C** for a printable version):

FIG 5.3   Kitiki and baloobah

Tell them that one of these shapes is called a 'kitiki' and the other is known as a 'baloobah'. (Decide for yourself which is which beforehand.) Point to the image on the left and ask the children how many of them think that this is the baloobah. Most of the children will put their hands up straight away. Then ask them how they decided.

As children answer, many of them will 'mould' the shape with their hands, telling you that baloobah sounds round and fluffy, or they may use comparisons such as 'it's like a cloud' or tell you about an association – that it sounds like 'balloon' etc. Then ask them to say why they thought the image on the right is the kitiki.

Once you've gone this far you can point out various interesting things to the class:

- The use of body language comes naturally to most people when they are speaking.

- We use our different senses to 'make sense' of some words we don't understand. In explaining kitiki and baloobah, children will use physical movement and multisensory words such as 'soft' (sound and touch) or 'round' (sound and visual).

- When we say 'baloobah', our mouths make a round shape and most of the work is done by the lips. When we say 'kitiki', our mouths are more stretched out and the tongue prods and jabs, picks and pokes at the teeth, while the back of the tongue presses against the palate.

- The baloobah shape is round and the word contains lots of round letters. The kitiki shape is spiky and sticky-out and so are the letters.

Now ask the class to think of some other baloobah-like words and kitiki-like words that are similar in some way. So you may get cloud, mound, globe, world, ball, round: spike, pin, stick, twig, nail, pick.

It may be sheer coincidence that many words denoting round things tend to use rounded letters while words that denote spiky things tend to use letters that 'stick out'. (Is it a coincidence that Baloo the Bear is the shape he is?) Some people think not.

Margaret Magnus is a programmer and linguist who, as she explains in her book *Gods in the word*, feels that many words carry *inherent meaning*; that certain meanings tend to be rooted in certain phonemes (distinct units of sound) because the evolution of language depends upon our physiology and the way we perceive the world. So for example, Magnus asserts that one sense of /str/- is linearity: string, strip, stripe, street. And one sense of -/ap/ is flatness: cap, flap, lap, map, etc. If you put them together, you get a flat line: strap.

Such connections can be extensive and subtle. Another phoneme that Magnus mentions is /gl/ – which has embedded within it the sense of light that is reflected or indirect as in glare, gleam, glim, glimmer, glint, glisten, glister, glitter, gloaming, glow.

While the theory of inherent meaning is controversial, Magnus' research is extensive and, to my mind, persuasive. The depth and scope of her ideas mean that we can only touch on the subject here. As a classroom activity however, you could ask children if they can match phonemes with word clusters that have some shared meaning, such as:

/b/ – round things; ball, balloon, bangle, bead, bell, berry, bladder, blimp, blister, blob, bowl, bracelet, bulb, bulge, button.
/g/ – gooiness; glob, glom, glop, gob, goo, gook, goop, goosh, gore, guck, gum, gunk.
/p/ – piercing; pick, pike, pin, pike, peck, prick, prong, prod.

A more light-hearted treatment of euphonics is to be found in John Michell's book of the same name, subtitled *A Poet's Dictionary of Enchantments*. Michell points out that the 'natural meaning' of sounds in words was discussed two thousand years ago in Plato's Cratylus and has been linked with the notion of enchantment – the magical influence of language – for far longer. It's not necessary to touch on that aspect of the subject to enjoy Michell's playful exploration of sounds.

For example, he asserts that /n/ carries the meaning of being 'inwardly denying' such that the sound often appears in words of negation; no, nay, non, nein, ne, niet, nada. He extends the idea to words denoting negative qualities, such as in those who are negative, niggling, nagging, narrow, nit-picking, snide, sneering and sneaky.

Soundscapes

Consolidate the children's learning by asking them to create 'sonic pictures' of busy scenes like a shopping centre, a fairground, a car boot sale etc. They can be in the form of descriptive paragraphs or list poems, as in James's piece 'Building Site':

Engines grinding
Dumpers clumping
Diggers dredging
Soil mountains tumbling and crumbling
Drills juddering, hammering and drrrrrrrrillllllllling!!
Metal clanging-banging
All around the clamour and the din –
Surveyors measuring – line of sight right
Girders towering
Dust blowing billowing dryly in the breeze
Smoke and chaos all around me
But as the scientist said,
'Out of clutter, find simplicity.' (Albert Einstein).

Nonsense words

As we have seen, our minds make sense of words at many levels. Even words that seem to have no referent can suggest meaning to us, as in 'baloobah' and 'kitiki' on page 75. We can still take pleasure from hearing and playing with such words even if it's simply a case of liking how they sound.

An equally if not more important aspect of playing with nonsense words is that they help us to feel more at ease with ambiguity and uncertainty. This is an important component of a writer's attitude towards their craft. The starting point for what may become a major piece of work might be the merest fragment of an idea. At that stage of the thinking process the writer will have very few answers – what counts is that they are willing to generate many questions.

Some children feel that they need to have 'all of the answers' at the outset. This is why when a child comes up with an idea and is then asked to say more, they will snatch any thought from out of the blue and use it without considering its usefulness or whether it works in terms of making a better story.

> **Top tip**
> Use an activity such as plot seeds on page 42 to highlight this point. Show the class one of the story ideas and be prepared to admit that, because you haven't thought about it yet, you don't know in any detail what will happen in the story or how it could turn out.

Accepting that no writer will know all of the answers at the start can be very reassuring and helps to boost a young writer's confidence when they are confronted with a 'cloud of unknowing'. Feeling comfortable with that, coupled with a repertoire of techniques for finding out more is highly empowering.

Playing with words can take many forms. At its most basic, wordplay is done to have fun with sounds and possible meanings that may be suggested. Nonsense words therefore are not 'non-words' as some official commentaries term them. If shared meaning can be assigned to a combination of letters then it becomes a legitimate word. Consider that not long ago words such as app, blog, bluetooth, sim, 3G, tweets, uplink, viner and voicemail were either nonsense words or words that did not exist in that combination (as in blue+tooth).

Top tip

Type 'glossary of computer terms' into your search engine to find even more great examples. I was delighted to come across:

- Captcha: A captcha is a challenge-response test that determines whether a user is human or an automated bot (bot itself being a new word, presumably a contraction of robot).
- Debugger: One who helps software developers to find and eliminate bugs while they are writing programs.
- Del.icio.us: Pronounced simply 'delicious', it is a community bookmarking website in which users can save Web pages they find and share them with other users.
- Kerning: This word refers to the spacing between the characters of a font.
- Netiquette: 'Net etiquette'. Good manners on the Internet.

One of the marvellous things about language is that it constantly grows and changes; as well as being beautiful in itself, language is ultimately a practical tool for reflecting our understanding of ourselves and the world. Today's nonsense words are legitimate members of tomorrow's lexicon.

So, let's do nonsense

For instance, show the class the word 'glombous'. Is it a nonsense word? Some children might understand that the –ous ending tags it as an adjective. More children might say that the 'glomb' makes it a baloobah-like word, while the 'gl' blend links it with stuff that is gloopy, gluey, globby, globe-like (globey?). So some sense has already been made out of it. It was never a 'non word' but, we might say, a *potential word*, a word-in-waiting.

Now ask the children to imagine that they are holding some glombous stuff in their hands. What does it feel like? How does it weigh? What happens when you squeeze it? What happens when you throw it at the wall? What might glombous stuff be useful for? If you had boots made from it would you galumph, galloop, gallub and glollop (but never gallop) along? If an alien was glombous, describe it in more detail. What kind of planet does it come from and what might that world be called?

Notice how this activity resembles the quick change trick on pages 31–32.

Take it further: Word clusters

Look back at the way some phonemes are associated with clusters of words (pages 75–77) and ask children to see if they can come up with nonsense words that share the connection. So for example (and according to Margaret Magnus) the phoneme /k/ (hard c) is often linked with marking or deforming a surface as in cut, crack, crop, cranny, crater, crease, crevasse, crinkle, crackle, crush. Nonsense words that exploit the association might be cropen (crack open), crunkle, crevissure (a crevice-like fissure), creese (verb, to crease repeatedly), cutackle (verb, to tackle the act of cutting so that it makes a crackling sound – trying to cut toffee brittle would make that sound).

Jabberwocky

In his famous poem, Lewis Carroll proved himself to be the master of nonsense words, or rather words-in-waiting that cry out for meaning to be assigned to them. From first hearing, brillig, slithy, toves, gyre, gimble etc. are rich with potential meaning, giving a new twist to T. S. Eliot's assertion that 'poetry can communicate before it is understood'.

Carroll himself suggested meanings for the words he invented. For example brillig (or bryllyg derived from the verb to bryl or broil) is the time of broiling dinner, i.e. the close of the afternoon. Slithy (or slythy, made up of slimy and lithe) means smooth and active. The proper pronunciation for the word uses a long 'i' (as in lithe) – according to www.waxdog.com/jabberwocky/def.html.

However, try them out with the children first. Ask the class what other words they are reminded of when they hear slithy, tove and gimble etc.

Top tip

If you show the words to the class before reading them the poem, they will not be influenced by the associations found in *Jabberwocky*.

So for slithy we might get someone who is sly and tells lies. Tove, a small treasure trove or, as a verb, to grub in loose soil or sand with your bare toes. Gimble, a trivial kind of gamble or to roll down the hill while laughing (a compound of giggle and tumble).

Take it further

Whether you use Carroll's invented words with *Jabberwocky* or not, ask the children to think of new words-in-waiting that might find a place in the poem. During one workshop we came up with reebs, grasting, swirlwind, decapedes, snoodled, houring, screamsome, breathly, gladeland, squeshy, opticus, gaart, sleez, dawnflower.

Top tip

As well as asking children to suggest the meanings of such words, you can use some of them to revisit the idea of parts of speech. 'Houring' for instance comes from 'hour' which is most commonly a noun, but here used as a verb (or adjective). Ask for suggestions for sentences using it in that way…

He spent all day houring away his time.

It was that violet-houring part of the evening.

The problem was long-houring before the solution occurred to him.

If you supply sentences such as these, ask the children to explain what they mean, 'translating' them into more conventional language.

Creative phonemics

Children are now routinely tested on their ability to recognise phonemes, both in the form of 'real' words and nonsense words ('non-words'). Whatever the arguments for or against such testing, wordplay in the various forms we have been looking at increases children's practical experience of recognising phonemes and so boosts their confidence when confronted by words that don't immediately (or never) make sense.

Nonsense words used in phonics assessment tests can't be shown to children beforehand of course, but to highlight the benefits of 'creative phonemics', you might have a go at giving some of them reasonable sounding definitions. For instance:

- Bim: onomatopoeia; the sound made by gently hitting your head against a thin sheet of metal. If you hit it harder it goes bam, harder still and it goes boom.
- Blan: a cooking implement that is a cross between a bowl and a pan. Various foods can be cooked in one including blancakes, blancmange and pigs in blankets. Almonds can also be blanched in a blan.
- Chom: onomatopoeia; the sound made during the chewing of a large morsel of food that is accidentally swallowed prematurely. The same sound is made when it comes back up as the Heimlich Manoeuvre is applied.
- Quemp: the sound a squirrel makes after eating too much fermented fruit and dropping into long grass from the branch on which it was trying to balance. The term has become generalised to include any instance of flopping bonelessly on to soft ground.
- Tox: half the sounds a clock makes.
- Ulf: noun; in Middle Earth an Ulf is an ugly elf.

Now have a go with – Blurst, Fape, Geck, Hild, Jound, Snemp, Spron, Steck, Stroft, Terg, Thazz, Tord, Vap, Voo.

Here are a few for the children to try out – Durd, Flomp, Glurp, Noib, Ong, Skalk, Splog, Twift, Yark.

Archaic words

Just as new words come into the language (go to www.oxforddictionaries.com for recent additions), others drop out of it or change their meanings, sometimes radically. Present the class with a selection of archaisms and ask the children to suggest possible meanings (whether or not you know the right answer yourself doesn't matter). Here are some examples with ideas for meanings from a Year 6 group (actual meanings in brackets):

- ague: to argue but not really lose your temper (malaria or a similar illness)
- apothecary: someone who carries pots full of broth (a person who prepared and sold medicine)
- beldam: a small stone tower on the wall of a dam containing a bell which is rung (by a beldammer) if the dam starts to leak (an old woman)
- bruit: a commanding instruction to make tea, as in 'Brew it!' (a report or rumour).

Here are a few more to try out for yourself or with the class:

- caducity
- ceil
- clew
- doit
- fainéant
- gyve
- kine
- nithing
- quidunc
- scaramoush (will you do the fandango!)
- sennight
- tweeny.

Some interesting changes of meaning are:

- aliment: originally food or nourishment
- audition: originally the power of hearing
- cadet: originally a younger son or daughter
- condition: originally a social position
- freak: originally a whim
- garland: originally a literary anthology
- halt: originally meaning lame
- learn: originally teach (that'll learn 'em!)
- measure: originally a dance
- reduce: originally to besiege and capture a town or fortress
- silly: originally helpless or defenceless
- speed: originally success, prosperity
- uncle: originally a pawnbroker
- usher: originally an assistant teacher(!).

Spoonerisms

A Spoonerism is a deliberate or accidental error of speech where consonants, vowels and morphemes (the smallest grammatical units of language) are switched around, usually between two words in a phrase. This type of wordplay (or mistake) is named after the Reverend Archibald Spooner (1844–1930) who was supposedly prone to making them. Various Spoonerisms have been attributed to him:

- The Lord is a shoving leopard (a loving shepherd)
- A blushing crow (crushing blow)
- A well-boiled icicle (well-oiled bicycle)
- You were fighting a liar in the quadrangle (lighting a fire)
- Is the bean dizzy? (Dean busy)

Trying to make up Spoonerisms can be difficult. The most effective way I know is to make a habit of playfully switching letters or syllables just to see what happens. Most of the combinations won't work, but occasionally you'll come up with a gem. Trying this out with different groups of children has produced:

- A mean gran (green man)
- As mean as custard (keen as mustard)
- Keys and parrots (peas and carrots)
- Mind your keys and pews (Ps and Qs)
- Wine feather (fine weather)
- Let's draw a sign in the land (line in the sand)
- Pips and cheese (chips and peas)

And, invented by the class teacher at break time in the staffroom (and applied only to small children), shiny tights.

Occasionally a Spoonerism acts as the seed of an idea for a story. Consider asking the class what kind of tales these would turn into:

- Bat casket (cat basket)
- Shaming of the true (taming of the shrew)
- Wee knights (week nights – not strictly a Spoonerism)

Playing with words in this way is great fun, but be warned it can become hobbit farming (habit forming!).

Take it further: Punning stories

A more difficult variation on the game is to take a proverb or a well known saying and play around with some of the words to create a new, and usually humorous, idea. So for instance 'You can lead a hearse to water but you cannot make it sink'.

For a real creative challenge, make the new proverb or saying part of a minisaga (see page 61) – a short story of exactly 50 words.

'The chicanery in the undertaking trade! Last month John Cadaver & Sons was caught bodysnatching from another firm. Yesterday they set a trap to force me into the lake. So thank goodness for my amphibious coffin-carrier, proving you can lead a hearse to water but you cannot make it sink.'

And one I'm particularly proud of –

'"Here woman!" Caractacus bellowed. "I will be battling the Romans soon. Fetch my blue warpaint, it's on the table amongst my trays of war-gear." Mandicartua rushed to carry out her husband's request, returning after long minutes empty handed.

"Apologies," she said, "But I can't see the woad for the trays."'

See what you and the children can make of these:

- I'm so angry I could heat a Norse (eat a horse)
- Beware of geeks sharing lifts (Greeks bearing gifts)
- A family hair loom (heirloom)
- Hand held imp lament (implement).

Top tip

Help children to create puns and Spoonerisms for themselves by running short brainstorming sessions. Using a saying like, 'There's no peace for the wicked', take key words and ask for homophones (same sounding) or words that sound similar to a greater or lesser degree. So peace would produce piece, pace, peuce, pose, while wicked could give us wicket, thicket, trick-it, rocket, socket. Then invite children to put to words together to produce the wordplay. The one that immediately occurred to me is, 'There's no piece for the wicket'. This gave me the punchline for the minisaga you'll find on page 61.

Malapropisms

A Malapropism, like a Spoonerism, can be deliberate or unintentional. It is the act or habit of misusing words such that a ridiculous outcome is created. Malapropisms are named after the character Mrs Malaprop in Sheridan's play *The Rivals* (1775), but are also known as Dogberryisms from Officer Dogberry, the name of a character in the Shakespeare play *Much Ado About Nothing*. 'Malaprop' incidentally comes from the French mal à propos meaning 'inappropriate'.

Again, it's quite a creative challenge to invent new Malapropisms, but the idea can form the basis of an enjoyable lesson showing children some already existing examples. These are readily available from the Internet and books such as *A Steroid Hit the Earth*, which also contains examples of misprints and typos – useful for sharpening up children's editing skills.

Two classic Malapropisms are:

- Mrs Malaprop said, "Illiterate him quite from your memory" (obliterate) and "She's as headstrong as an allegory." (alligator)
- Officer Dogberry said, "Our watch, sir, have indeed comprehended two auspicious persons." (apprehended two suspicious persons)

Some others, which amused me anyway, are:

- Alice said she couldn't eat crabs or any other crushed Asians. (crustaceans)
- A rolling stone gathers no moths. (moss)
- Professor Brain is a great suppository of knowledge. (repository)
- He stood putrefied with horror. (petrified)
- Taking the prawn won him the chess game. (pawn)
- Orion is one of the most well known constipations. (constellations)

Finally, I came across a couple of delightful word confusions in schools I visited recently. One appeared in the journal of a Year 6 girl who was writing about her recent induction day at the local secondary – 'And after break Mrs Harries showed us the new computers they had in the icy tea room.' Another child wrote 'None of the children were at school on Monday because the teachers had an insect day.'

Puns

These are usually deliberate plays on words for humorous effect that exploit different possible meanings of words or make use of words that sound the same but have different meanings (homophones).

- Waiters at the local Indian restaurant try hard to curry favour with their regular customers.
- Doctor Frankenstein's assistant was always Igor to please.
- The sailor's motto was 'Do it schooner rather than later!'
- Wrestling with the lion was scary, but I decided to feel the fur and do it anyway.
- I hadn't prepared for my lecture on garden birds so decided to wing it. It went well. I wrote a tweet about it afterwards.
- Tony wanted to be a plumber but his Mum thought it was only a pipe dream.
- I'm trying to watch my weight so I thought, should I buy yoghurt or bacon? I decided that buying the bacon was rasher.
- My new penpal in Moscow sent me a box of bacon on my birthday. It was a case of from rasher with love. (I invented that one myself. You might say it's home-groan.)

Some puns are unintentional. Ask children to be on the lookout for these. Two that I came across while writing this chapter are:

'Allergy advice. Loose nuts on sale in the store.'

And in a news item reporting a new Apple update, 'Apple has also removed apps for its new health software because of a bug'.

As a classroom activity, after showing the children various puns, give them pairs of similar sounding words to see if they can come up with some of their own – reason/raisin, pause/paws, bear/bare, I/eye, cell/sell, fair/fare, mail/male etc.

Look both ways

'Compressed' sentences such as those found on signs and as newspaper headlines are sometimes ambiguous insofar as they can be read in two or more ways, just as the famous box illusion tempts the mind to see it first one way then another.

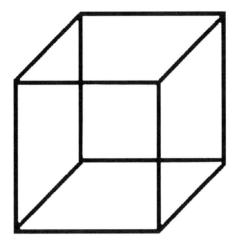

FIG 5.4   Box illusion

Show the class some vaguely worded or ambiguous sentences. Being able to toggle between alternative meanings exercises the mental muscles and helps children to 'read between the lines' when confronted with more sophisticated messages. Here are some to begin with:

- Dog for sale: eats anything and is fond of children
- Now is your chance to have your ears pierced and get an extra pair to take home too
- Have several very old dresses from grandmother in beautiful condition
- Dogs must be carried on escalators!
- Slow children at play
- Watch batteries fitted here
- *In a clothing shop:* Wonderful bargains for men with 16 and 17 necks
- *Seen in a laundrette:* Automatic washing machines – please remove all your clothes when the light goes out
- *And, cruelly*: Illiterate? Write today for free help.

Headlines:

- Kids make nutritious snacks
- Stolen painting found by tree
- Red tape holds up new bridge

- Nurses help dog bite victim
- If strike isn't settled quickly, it may last a while
- Safety experts say school bus passengers should be belted.

Tom Swifties

A Tom Swifty is a kind of pun that links what Tom says with the way that he says it. The name comes from the central character of a series of Science Fiction books which first appeared in 1910 and which have continued to be written by various authors (under the collective pseudonym of Victor Appleton) up to present times.

Apart from being good fun, inventing Tom Swifties is a useful way of introducing or revisiting verbs, -ly adverbs and adverbial phrases.

- "I'm no good at playing darts," Tom said aimlessly.
- "I've struck oil!" Tom yelled crudely.
- "I forgot what I was supposed to buy," Tom admitted listlessly.
- "I can't find the bananas," Tom muttered fruitlessly.
- "How do I get to the cemetery?" Tom asked gravely.
- "Get that dog off my lawn!" Tom barked.
- "Well *I* didn't mislay the soap," Tom said, washing his hands of the whole affair.
- "I must sharpen my pencil," Tom declared bluntly. "I've sharpened it now," he added, coming straight to the point.

And my personal favourite:

- "I think I've developed a split personality," Tom said, being frank.

For more information on parts of speech and writing style see for example Ben Yagoda's book *When You Catch an Adjective, Kill It: The Parts of Speech, for Better And/Or Worse*.

These activities demonstrate the link between humour and creativity. A quick Internet search will pull up many articles and references reinforcing the notion that a healthy sense of humour – which often picks out fresh, unusual and quirky links between ideas – correlates strongly with higher level creative thinking, two key elements of which are:

- making connections
- looking at things in a variety of ways.

It's also true that you can't laugh and be stressed at the same time. A classroom environment that allows and indeed encourages humour, that values thinking and the tolerance of ambiguity and uncertainty ('But how can we find out?') boosts children's self-confidence, raises their self-esteem and enhances their capacity to learn – and to learn how to learn.

Chapter 6
Building storytelling skills

'What shall we tell you? Tales, marvellous tales of ships and stars and isles where good men meet'. James Elroy Flecker, author

It might seem that standing in front of an audience to tell a story would be one of the most terrifying experiences you could inflict on a child and hardly one to build his self-confidence. However, within a nurturing environment, armed with some techniques for dealing with feelings and having cultivated a love of words, many children will be happy to have a go at your suggestion. In the same way that a community of writers makes writing less daunting, so a community of storytellers will support and encourage each other.

Introduce the idea with these key points:

– We all tell stories naturally, if only in the form of anecdotes, gossip and chit chat (see the 'Ladder to the Moon' on page 90). Learning to tell a story more formally is simply building on skills we already possess.
– Learning to tell stories develops a range of interpersonal and communication skills that will be valuable in other areas of learning and in life generally.
– Telling a story – and knowing you have done it will – is a very enjoyable and fulfilling experience (both for the teller and the listeners).
– Becoming a more accomplished storyteller boosts self-confidence and forms a valuable addition to your list of achievements.

The value of stories

As well as the benefits listed above, preparing a story for telling and then recounting it:

– creates shared quality time in the classroom
– encourages children to ask questions and cultivates curiosity
– engages interest and attention, develops concentration
– develops active imagination
– increases children's vocabulary
– develops understanding of story structure
– gives experience and teaches tolerance of other people's viewpoints, lives and cultures
– can spark inspiration for greater ventures in life
– cultivates a greater ability to flourish in 'a world of words'
– and, in terms of understanding narrative itself, helps children to make sense of the world through narrative templates.

In addition, the process creates an opportunity for young storytellers to rehearse roles, rules, rights and responsibilities vicariously through story. Such experiences help children to understand the viewpoints and feelings of others, which in turn serves to increase children's 'emotional intelligence'. It allows for positive inspiration through the presence of hero figures, their quests and the challenges those adventures bring. Heroes traditionally embody noble human qualities yet are themselves essentially mortal and therefore vulnerable. Heroism as such, even in something as everyday as plucking up the courage to speak to someone you don't know, is a real phenomenon open to everyone. Telling hero tales opens doorways of possibility in children's imaginations.

Preparing and telling stories also develops metaphorical/symbolic thinking and leads to greater understanding of the world.

A hierarchy of understandings

Kieran Egan, Faculty Member in Education at Simon Fraser University in Canada, proposes that as we grow we move through a 'hierarchy of understandings' that allow us to relate to and make sense of the world in various ways. Our earliest understanding (in the sense of experiencing and becoming acquainted with things) is body-oriented or what Egan calls 'somatic understanding'. This is expressed often in polar opposites of hot/cold, hungry or thirsty/satisfied, upset/happy etc. Subsequently, as children we understand the world 'mythically'. There is much that seems mysterious to us and we have not yet acquired any great knowledge and experience of the world, and so we make up possible explanations and stories to satisfy our need to make sense of our lives. This propensity for 'myth making' is fed by nursery stories, folk-tales, picture books, comics and TV that we are exposed to.

Subsequently, we move into a phase of 'romantic understanding' where older children are armed with emergent conscious critical faculties. Here perhaps they recognize the naiveté of their myths; certainly the stories must be refined as knowledge and conscious ability increase. Romantic understanding is still driven by a sense of wonder (an essential motivation for all enquiry) but this is moderated by the need to find limits and boundaries; to create paradigms that act as frameworks for further experience.

Adult understanding is 'philosophic' in Egan's terminology – ideally based on learning, knowledge and greater experience. Such an understanding is also highly conceptual. We make sense of the world through a complex and sophisticated web of ideas, which amounts to our lifelong interpretation of what we experience (i.e. the so-called map of reality).

Such a web of ideas can also snare us however if we are not prepared to consider new perspectives. If we are set in our ways of understanding, we can suffer what has been called a 'hardening of the categories'. Here we become resistant to new ideas and are increasingly convinced that our way of looking at the world is the 'right' way. This kind of mental hardening also stifles creative thought.

Fortunately, Kieran Egan identifies a further understanding beyond the philosophic, which he calls 'ironic understanding'. Such understanding is flexible, playful, exploratory, challenging, and sometimes mischievous – in the same way as the mythical Trickster archetype brings a subversive energy to human attempts to explain the world. Ironic understanding embodies two key elements of creativity: the ability to in-form oneself, to make mental links that have not been made before; and the ability to look at concepts, problems, and so on, from a range of perspectives.

Stories provide an ideal means of helping children to move along the hierarchy of understandings. A story presents us with vicarious experiences, opening up new and perhaps previously unimagined possibilities. In many ways stories can also 'tell us something true'. This can happen at a deep structural level, such as allowing us to understand the nature of heroism and to begin to see its presence in ourselves, but also in 'teaching tales' such as fables and parables. In this sense myths are much more than stories that just aren't true (that connotation evolved around the mid-1800s): they represent templates and guidelines full of wisdom about how we might best live our lives.

Reference: *The Educated Mind*.

Bloom's taxonomy of thinking skills

This idea is relatively well known in education and is the brainchild of educational psychologist Benjamin Bloom. Bloom's model identifies various modes of thinking that lead from simple thinking coupled with little understanding, to advanced thinking leading to and allied with greater understanding of the world. His original taxonomy was:

- Knowledge: knowing and remembering; repeating, defining, identifying, telling who, when, which, where, what.

- Comprehension: describing in your own words; telling how you feel (interpreting and understanding) about it, what it means, explaining, comparing, relating.

- Application: applying, making use of; what you know, using it to solve problems, demonstrating understanding.

- Analysis: taking apart, being critical; the causes/problems/solutions/consequences.

- Synthesis: connecting, being creative; speculating, putting together, developing, improving, creating and inventing.

- Evaluation: judging and assessing; expressing preferences backed by reasons.

(See Rockett & Percival's *Thinking for Learning* for a more in-depth explanation.)

Bloom's taxonomy was built on earlier work by Piaget and Vygotsky that suggested thinking skills and capacities are developed by cognitive challenge. Again, stories provide a rich and practical context for making children aware of these evolving ways of thinking. When they write their own stories as much as when they prepare a story for telling, encourage children to explore through questioning:

- Knowledge: What happened in the story?

- Comprehension: Why did it happen that way?

- Application: What would you have done? Why do you think the author did it that way?

- Analysis: Which part did you like best, etc., and why?

- Synthesis: Can you think of a different ending? Can you modify the story? Can you create a new story of your own?

- Evaluation: What did you think of the story? Why? Justify your opinions with reasons.

Finally, teaching children how to tell stories consolidates many of the ideas and activities mentioned in the previous sections of this book by providing an enjoyable context for utilising the raft of skills you are helping to develop.

The ladder to the moon

This is a powerful and poetical image of a ladder rising from the earth and leaning against the moon to represent not just the idea that there exists a hierarchy of stories, from the mundane to the numinous or 'cosmic', but also the universality of stories, their connectedness to each other and the fact that they are told across the world and have been since humans first appeared. The image also represents the idea that our history and sense of belonging are grounded in the earth – in the ordinary and the everyday – but our imaginations, aspirations and most profound sense of who we are also find meaning in the heavens and 'the grand scheme of things'.

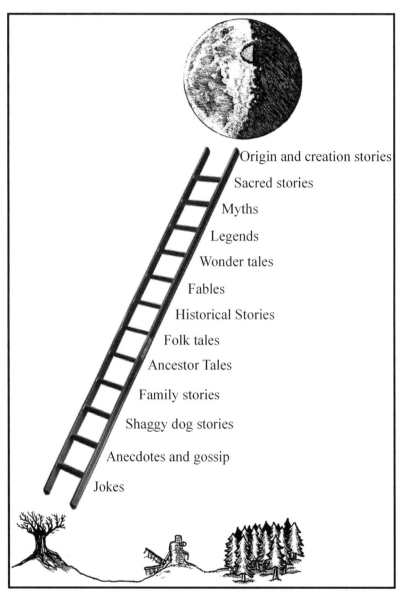

FIG 6.1   Ladder to the moon, see Bloomsbury Online Resource 6A

You may want simply to introduce the idea of the ladder to the moon as a way of allowing children to understand that even playground chatter counts as 'story' and that the telling of tales of one sort or another goes on everywhere. It is a natural part of what makes us human and civilised and is therefore to be valued. You can also use the image as the basis of a wall display, asking the class to find examples of the different kinds of stories that exist. See **Bloomsbury Online Resource 6A** for a printable version.

A traditional epithet from Siberia says that 'If you don't know the trees you may be lost in the forest, but if you don't know the stories you may be lost in life.' Helping children to become familiar with a greater range of stories, and showing them how to become better at creating their own, therefore counts as one of the most important cornerstones of their education.

First steps

Earlier I suggested 'modelling the behaviour' by writing yourself when you ask the children to write. This reinforces the notion of your class being a community of writers and gives children more confidence to have a go, especially when you share with them the difficulties and frustrations you experienced in trying to make the story work.

The same pedagogical point applies to preparing and telling a story. Go through the process yourself, using your story not so much as an example of 'the way to do it', but to test out your chosen process (one strategy is suggested below) and as a way of demonstrating the value you place on storytelling *per se*.

Before asking children to select and prepare a story, you may consider discussing the following points with them:

- What makes a good story?
- Why do we tell stories?
- What are the differences between a written story and one that is told?
- How can you use your voice to engage and audience?
- How can you use body language to help tell a story?
- How can you adapt a well known/traditional story?

Use Merlin!

With regard to the last point, there is a mental tool that will help children to generate ideas quickly for changing traditional stories.

Explain to the class that Merlin is 'the wizard of our imagination' and that by waving his wand he can make things change in all kinds of interesting ways.

Take a well known story to demonstrate the technique, for example Cinderella.

The usual ways that Merlin can transform something is by:

- making bigger
- making smaller
- taking something away
- 'stretching' something
- turning something around
- swapping something.

These ideas are deliberately vague to allow 'creative space' for children to apply them in different ways. So for instance 'making bigger' could translate into Cinderella having an even longer list of chores to do, having more than two step sisters, making the Prince's party an even grander affair, etc. One child had the idea of creating 'The Adventures of Cinderella' – a series of short stories about the same character.

If children struggle in applying the Merlin technique to a story, guide them by pointing out the most obvious things that can be changed; plot, characters, settings, objects.

Establishing story time in your classroom

- If you can, share and tell stories at a regular time and in the same place.
- Commit yourself to it. Once you introduce story time, stick with it.
- Decide on the length of the session and make this a rule.
- Use the sharing time to find out more about your child's day. Ask questions about this at opportune times in the session.

Tips for telling a story:

1. Choose a story that you like (whether you've written it yourself or are using someone else's).
2. Stories don't have to be long and involved. They can be short and simple and in fact it's better to start with these.
3. Think about the differences between a written story and one that's told.
4. Match the story you pick to the age of the audience.
5. Break the story down into short sections. This will help you to remember the sequence of events.
6. Write out the story in your own words or create a story plan like the one on page 93.

The plan can be as rough and sketchy as the example shown. What matters is the visual organisation of the ideas, not the quality of the artwork.

FIG 6.2   Story plan

7. Tell the story to yourself out loud, using your notes as a guide. You might then have a go at telling the story again without notes to a friend.

8. Keep the language plain and simple. Use some vivid descriptive details to bring characters and places alive. Your audience will fill in lots of other details for themselves – they have good imaginations too.

9. Use facial expression, body language and mime to enrich your storytelling.

10. There's no need to memorise a story; just have a sense of where the plot is going and be prepared to improvise.

11. Imagine what's happening in your story and tell it as you see it.

12. Practise telling the story out loud to a few friends before you present it to the audience.

13. Involve the audience. Include everyone using eye contact. If you can, build audience reaction into your story.

14. Remember there's a difference between you as the narrator of the story and pretending to be the characters in it. If you decide to become the characters, give each of them at least one special characteristic.

15. Take your time. Don't rush to finish. Enjoy telling your story and your listeners will enjoy it more too.

A plan for storytelling

The educational benefits of storytelling I have tried to highlight are intended to demonstrate that it should not be considered as a peripheral item on the syllabus to be fitted in when time allows, nor is it in any way a 'luxury' to be indulged in when the 'real learning' has been covered.

Having said that, a storytelling project can take many forms and fit into any reasonable time frame. You may already have the skills as a storyteller to demonstrate some techniques for the children to practise. Alternatively there are many clips on sites like YouTube that show storytellers in action, plus tutorials on how to develop storytelling skills. Ideally (though I may be accused of touting for business), invite a professional storyteller or author/storyteller into the school. The children will then see a live performance of what good storytelling looks like. Additionally, the guest author will be able to give practical tips on writing, flag up the benefits of developing the skills of writing and communicate his or her love of language in the most powerful way. In short, an author will radiate enthusiasm while embodying the ethos that I have tried to define throughout this book.

Usually authors/storytellers are invited into a school for a day. Such a visit can kickstart a storytelling and/or creative writing project, though seeing it through will be left to you. I suspect that most authors won't object to their storytelling sessions and talks being filmed, so creating a lasting resource for the school. Sometimes authors are asked to be 'writers in residence' over half a term or longer. This gives them and you scope to develop a more robust plan for a storytelling or writing project where the author will be available to review and feed back ideas throughout the process.

While you might choose to launch a storytelling project just with your own class, the option also exists for colleagues to involve themselves in a plan on a grander scale. Recently I was invited to Bemrose School in Derby to take part in a storytelling day that involved an entire year group (180 Year 9s, though the scheme would work equally well at primary level).

Obviously the day was highly structured and thoroughly planned beforehand.

Venue: school hall for author sessions/performances, nearby classrooms for group work.

- Introductory talk by author followed by Q&A session, 30 minutes.
- Storytelling session by author, 30 minutes.

- Analysis and discussion of storytelling techniques, 30 minutes. This also involved jotting down insights on sticky notes and posting them up.
- Students split into groups to choose a story to prepare for telling. Groups could use a story already told by the author (adapting it as required), use a well known traditional tale, or create a story for themselves, planning and structuring it not for writing but for telling as the first and primary outcome, 60 minutes.
- Rehearsal of story tellings, 45 minutes. Stories could be performed by a group (thus looking more like a piece of drama), or told such that different students took responsibility for different sections of the story. Individual students could opt for solo performances. No student was made to do a telling.
- Selected groups returned to the hall to have their performances filmed, 30 minutes. The other groups remained in classrooms to do their storytellings there.
- All students and staff in the hall to watch the (partially edited) footage of the filmed performances, 15 minutes. Round off and celebrate the day.

Such a day was intensive, as you might imagine, though the feedback from students was very positive, and staff felt that the time, effort and money had been well spent.

Sample stories for telling

Here are a few short stories that you might want to tell (as opposed to just reading them out). Alternatively, you can use them with the children to help develop their own storytelling skills. Feel free to alter the text in any way in light of the points made earlier. For more stories in an editable format, see **Bloomsbury Online Resource 6B**.

*

But Mum, There's a Monster Upstairs!

Neil Stern was sitting quietly watching the television. Suddenly his father yawned a huge yawn. "Oh, I'm tired out," Mr Stern said.

"So am I," added Neil's Mum. She yawned too, but both of them were determined to stay up to finish watching the programme on the TV.

Neil didn't want to go to bed yet either, as he was enjoying the programme too. (He knew he could record it to watch tomorrow, but he hated going to bed this early!) So he snuggled a cushion close to him, pulled the throw around himself and squeezed into the smallest space he could make…

BUT – "Time for bed, Neil," Mrs Stern said rather sternly a moment later.

"Oh Mum, can't I stay up and –"

"No," Neil's Mum made a scowly face.

"Finish watching this programme –"

"No." Neil's Dad sounded even sterner this time.

"On the television?"

"No!" both of his parents said together, very *very* sternly this time.

Neil gave a long, sad sigh. He struggled out of the throw (making more of a fuss about this than he needed to) and pushed his cushion away before slowly and grumpily slouching out of the room.

A minute later he came back and peered around the living room door. "Dad, it's dark up the stairs."

"I'll switch the light on, then," Mr Stern got up from his armchair, went into the hall and switched on the landing light.

"And now," Mr Stern told Neil, "get yourself off to bed and go to sleep!"

"Yes Dad," Neil said quietly, closing the door behind him.

Two minutes later he opened it again and peeped around at his parents.

"Mum, it's dark in the bathroom."

"Why don't you switch the light on then?" Mr Stern wondered.

"I can't find the cord in the dark." That sounded feeble even to Neil. He wondered if his Mum and Dad would show pity on him even so and let him stay up.

But instead… "I'll switch the light on then," Mrs Stern said. She got out of her armchair, went up the stairs and switched on the bathroom light before coming straight back down to watch her programme, though she paused in the hallway long enough to call out, "Now get yourself off to bed Neil and go to sleep!"

"Yes Mum," Neil answered meekly.

Three minutes later Neil peeked around the living room door again. He saw his parents glance at each other and sigh.

"Mum… Dad…" Neil began.

"What now?" Mr Stern wondered, trying out his grumpiest frown. "Is it dark in your bedroom too?"

"No," Neil replied, "there's a monster upstairs."

"Is there really?" Mr Stern did not seem bothered one bit.

"Yes. It's big and purple and it has bright green spots."

"I'm sure it's harmless Neil," his mother told him patiently.

"And it's *bound* to be going home soon," Mr Stern added. "Even monsters don't stay up much later than this."

Neil glanced at the television set. "Well as long as it's still up there, can I finish watching…"

"No!" yelled his parents, both at the same time.

"that programme…"

"No!!"

"…on the TV? Only until the monster goes away?" he added quickly, before clumping back up the stairs to show what a bad mood he was in.

Four minutes later, Neil peered around the living room door again. "Mum…"

"What now?" snapped Mrs Stern. "Don't tell me that monster is still there?" She smiled at her husband, but the smile vanished as she looked at Neil. "Get to bed. How many times do we have to tell you!"

"But Mum, I've come to say that now there are *two* monsters upstairs."

"Is that so?" Mrs Stern wondered. "They're probably friends."

"Yes, and the other one is blue with bright yellow stripes."

"For the last time Neil go to bed," his father told him wearily, "and go to sleep."

"Yes Dad," Neil said, trying to make his voice sound like a little puppy-whimper.

Five minutes later the living room door opened very slowly and Neil's nose appeared a few seconds before the rest of his face. "Mum, Dad…"

"Don't tell me," Mr Stern interrupted him. He was starting to smile despite himself. "There's *another* monster upstairs now. That makes three!"

"And this one has got lots of pink tentacles," Mrs Stern giggled.

"And six red eyes and an orange head!" Mr Stern added, chuckling.

"And they're all having a party," Neil's mother went on, bursting into peals of laughter, "in your bedroom!"

Mr Stern gave a great bellow of mirth and slapped his hands on his thighs as he rocked backwards and forwards in his armchair.

Neil looked puzzled. "How do you know?"

His parents, rolling about in their chairs, wiped the tears from their eyes and looked fondly at their son, shaking their heads at his antics.

"Because we were once children as well Neil," Mrs Stern explained.

Mr Stern added, "And we always wanted to stay up late to watch the television too."

"So we used to make up the most wonderful excuses for our parents. But they never believed us either."

"No," Mr Stern said, "they <u>never</u> believed us. So get yourself off to bed now and go to sleep."

"Oh all right," Neil said in a small defeated voice. The television programme was finishing now anyway. "I'll say goodnight then – Goodnight then."

"Goodnight, son," his parents said as Neil closed the living room door, climbed the stairs, went into his bedroom, scrambled into his bed and pulled the blankets up right over his head.

Oh well, Neil thought. It was a good try I suppose.

He closed his eyes, but they wouldn't stay closed because the purple monster with bright green spots was doing the jive.

The blue monster with bright yellow stripes was doing the cha-cha.

And the monster with pink tentacles, six purple eyes and an orange head was doing the waltz with Neil's dressing gown as a partner.

Neil grinned at their antics and presently jumped out of bed to join in too.

Well, I did go to bed like Mum and Dad told me, he thought. But it will be a little while yet before I can get off to sleep.

*

A Mighty Leap

Like I said, even though Nigel Lloyd was one of the smallest kids in the school he was the boss of the Double Darers. This was partly because he could think of the best dares. Also, if you wanted to join the group you had to pass a Test of Courage. When I wanted to join, my Test of Courage was to run across the flat roof of a garage and jump a five-foot gap on to the next roof. Up the lane where we hang out there was this row of garages, but they'd been built separately with gaps between.

I watched Nige climb up on to the garage, hurtle across the roof and leap lightly over the gap. I thought, 'I can do that,' but I was bigger and heavier than Nige. And when I clambered up onto that roof I saw that it was made from sheets of corrugated iron – old, rusty sheets of corrugated iron.

As I clattered and clanged my way across that roof the whole thing was bouncing and swaying, creaking and groaning… I thought that it was all going to collapse, so that I'd drop down into the garage and get covered in rubble and end up in hospital!

I was so nervous about it that I mistimed my jump and fell between the garages!

On the way down I banged my head, cracked my elbow, knocked my knee, tore my shirt, muddied my trousers, scuffed my shoes and landed face-down – SPLAT – in a puddle of dirty water at the bottom…

I came out from between those two garages looking like the Mud Monster and just stood there dripping. I hurt all over, but I hurt most of all inside because I'd failed to do the jump.

Well, Nigel came up to me with a big grin on his face, his hand held out.

"Congratulations," he said, "welcome to the Double Darers – oh, no I won't shake your hand you've got doggy poo on it."

"But Nige," I said, wiping the poo on the grass, "look at me, I've made a mess of everything."

"Uh-uh." He shook his head. "You dared to do it and you did your best."

That was one of the two main mottoes of the Double Darers – Dare to do it and do your best. Also, 'Have fun but hurt no one (including yourself if you can help it).'

Pretty good advice in all kinds of ways if you ask me.

*

Oomph!

Professor Tom Taylor was an inventor.

Once he invented a book that read to itself.

Once he invented an apple that tasted of any fruit you liked.

Once he invented a wristwatch that reminded you when to do things.

And yesterday he invented a new drink called Oomph!

Oomph was blue and fizzy and looked a bit unusual.

"Hmm, tastes rather like lemonade," Professor Taylor said. After that, he cleaned the whole house in two minutes flat. Because, you see, Oomph was what Professor Taylor called a pick-me-up. It gave you more energy, more oomph – it let you do things a little bit faster than usual.

At least, that was the idea.

Unfortunately, Professor Taylor put too much zest and <u>much</u> too much zip and whiz into his first batch of Oomph.

Not only that, but he managed to spill some too…

One drop fell on to a bee that was buzzing through the room at the time. It went shooting away like a bullet, bouncing off the walls and ceiling, whisking through cobwebs, dive-bombing the cat. Then it attacked the vase of flowers and drank down all the nectar in a flash!

Crash! Tinkle! went the window as the bee smashed through and vanished into the distance.

"Wow," said Professor Taylor, "that's powerful stuff!"

He gave a little smile… But the smile sagged as he noticed the family's new kitten (it was named Caboodle) licking some of the spilled Oomph.

Instantly Caboodle's fur went whoosh! and stood on end, her whiskers stuck out – boing! – like bristles and her tail spun round like helicopter blades.

She suddenly moved at super-speed, running around the walls, swinging on the lampshade, clinging to the ceiling like a spider. Caboodle's eyes were wide and her ears were pinned back. She wore a big mad smile and seemed to be enjoying herself.

"I'm going on a mouse safari," she told Professor Taylor, although all he heard was 'Meaow me-me-prreow – meeeooowww!'

And Caboodle was gone.

"Goodness gracious, " Professor Taylor started to say. Then Caboodle was back with a fruit basket containing twenty-three rather surprised looking mice (Professor Taylor let them all escape later).

"Gosh, I'm tired out," Caboodle said. She curled up on the chair and slept for three whole seconds before zooming away again to play in the garden.

"Well," said Professor Taylor. "Well, well, well…" And he gave a sly little chuckle, because he'd just had an idea.

He looked at the Oomph that was left in the glass he'd knocked over. He thought about it. He thought about it again. Then he picked up the glass and drank some Oomph down.

Nothing much happened and Professor Taylor was ever so faintly disappointed.

"Oh dear," he sighed, "I was hoping that at least I'd feel a bit more lively." Then suddenly, "Aaaahhh! Wheeeee!"

He exploded into action. His hair and eyebrows went <u>crinkle</u> and grew very long. He seemed to burst with energy.

"Right, let's get to it then!" he said so quickly that it sounded like 'Rn!' And he was off.

He tidied the garage and shed, did all the washing up, cleaned the car, mowed the lawn, ironed all the clothes, cooked the tea, read three books, wrote fifteen letters, played with the cat, did some exercises, decorated the spare bedroom, went for a bike ride and then clipped his nails – all in five minutes.

Meanwhile Tom Taylor's wife Tanya Taylor had been out shopping. Wearily she pushed open the creaky garden gate and dragged herself up the path.

"Oh," she said, "I'm so tired. All I want to do is…"

Without any warning a whirlwind zoomed out of the house, tidied up some fallen leaves, took Mrs Taylor's shopping bags from her, disappeared back into the house, reappeared dressed in some smart dancing clothes and said, "There's nothing left to do here darling so let's PARTY-Y-Y-Y-Y!"

Mrs Taylor started to shake her head and say "No," but Professor Taylor popped some drops of Oomph into her mouth. And –

She showered and dressed in ten seconds. Then they hit the town.

They went shopping.

They ate a Chinese meal very quickly.

They saw the sights.

They went to a night club and danced and danced and danced until dawn.

Then they ran home and whirled into their sparkling clean lounge and – then – slowed – down – and – slumped – into – the – armchairs…

"That was really good fun," Professor Taylor said heavily. "We must do it again – some – timezzzzz…"

And he was asleep.

"Yes dear…" Mrs Taylor was dozing off too.

"But not until this afternoon, eh?"

*

End words

The American essayist Ralph Waldo Emerson said that 'To be yourself in a world that is constantly trying to make you something else is the greatest accomplishment'.

At the heart of this book lies the observation that a child's lack of confidence and low self-esteem are often the result of other people's actions, comments and judgements. These happen for a raft of reasons, not least of which is the commentator's wish to inflate his own ego, belittling others to make himself look bigger. Children who allow themselves to be influenced by negative judgements often fall into the habit of creating negative *self* judgements, which can lead in the end to a 'confidence crisis'.

It's important for children to realise, however much they struggle with their writing, that writers never stop learning. Every word is a further step towards gaining greater mastery of the craft. More than that, when a child has produced a piece of work through his own efforts he can feel justly pleased with the achievement of bringing something new and unique into the world, however roughly formed it is due to being a product of that child's current stage of development. A story, a poem, a journal or diary extract, all reflect the viewpoint of that individual and help others to understand his world picture. From the writer's point of view, having a vehicle to express one's thoughts and feelings in such an immediate and creative way can be immensely satisfying and a powerful positive influence on his mental/emotional health and wellbeing.

The activities I've written about are designed to help children take more control of their thoughts and feelings, so that they can feel empowered to be more fully and authentically themselves, coupled with the realisation that fulfilment of potential is the result of creative thought, effort, discipline and much self reflection.

While the focus has been on writing, primarily within the classroom, the techniques and strategies can apply in all areas of a child's life. And while the intention is that children will become better writers as a result of practising these techniques, ideally they will also become more creative, independent, self-confident and useful members of the community; qualities that radiate out to influence others in a positive way for, as the old proverb advises us, 'work on yourself and serve the world'.

Bibliography

Bowkett, S. et al (2008) *Happy Families: insights into the art of parenting*, London: Network Continuum. (Contains chapters on story sharing and story telling.)

Bowkett, S. (2009) *Countdown to Creative Writing*, Abingdon, Oxon: Routledge.

Bowkett, S. (2010) *Developing Literacy and Creative Writing Through Storymaking*, Maidenhead: Open University Press.

Bowkett, S. (2014) *A Creative Approach to Teaching Writing*, London: Bloomsbury.

Briers, S. (2009) *Brilliant Cognitive Behavioural Therapy*, Harlow: Pearson Education.

Dweck, C. (2000) *Self-Theories: Their Role in Motivation, Personality and Development*. London: Taylor and Francis.

Dweck, C. (2012) *Mindset. London: Robinson*

Egan, K. (1992) *Imagination in Teaching and Learning: ages 8–15*, London: Routledge.

Egan, K. (1998) *The Educated Mind: how cognitive tools shape our understanding*, Chicago & London: University of Chicago Press.

Gardner, H. (2006) *Multiple Intelligences: New Horizons in Theory and Practice*, New York: Basic Books.

Magnus, M. (2010) *Gods in the Word*, CreateSpace.com, ISBN 9781453824443.

McGuinness, D. (1998) *Why Children Can't Read: and what we can do about it*, London: Penguin.

Michell, J. (2006) *Euphonics: a poet's dictionary of enchantments*, Glastonbury: Wooden Books.

Neenan, M. & Dryden, W. (2004) *Cognitive Therapy*, Hove & New York: Brunner-Routledge.

Rockett, M. & Percival, S. (2002) *Thinking for Learning*, Stafford: Network Educational Press.

Rose, C. (1991) *Accelerated Learning*, Aylesbury, Bucks: Accelerated Learning Systems Ltd.

Toseland, M. (2008), *A Steroid Hit The Earth*, London: Portico Books.

Truss, L. (2003), *Eats, Shoots & Leaves: the zero tolerance approach to punctuation*, London: Profile Books.

Index